# UKULELE FC BEGINNERS AND BEYOND

A Complete Music Method and Songbook for Kids and Adults

### PIERRE HACHÉ MUSIC

**Pierrehachemusic.com**

**Author and Interior Design:** Pierre Haché
**Editor:** Heather Jamieson
**Cover Design:** Eoin Hickey
**Photography:** Lily Brender-Haché

ISBN: 978-1-9992059-6-6
Copyright © 2022 Pierre Haché

A heartfelt THANK YOU to everyone who was involved in the creation of this ukulele method and to my teachers and students who helped shape its contents.

# AUTHOR'S NOTE

Not only is playing music tons of fun, it helps develop focus, discipline and creativity. I truly hope these pages will help bring the JOY of music into the lives of its readers, young and old.

First of all, this project would not be possible without the help of a small, but very talented team. A special thanks to my invaluable editor, Heather Jamieson, for her thoroughness, passion and commitment to my books. And a huge thank you to my brilliant designer Eoin Hickey, for his incredible skill, patience and professionalism.

**Ukulele For Beginners and Beyond** is a companion book to my first ukulele method, **Easy Ukulele**, which emphasized strumming and singing. Including popular songs from The Beatles to Bob Marley, it has been a huge success and has brought the satisfaction of making music to thousands.

This second book will not only add to your repertoire of songs to strum and sing, it will also teach you how to play 30 well-known melodies. Filled with pictures and diagrams, this easy-to-follow method teaches the basics of reading rhythm, musical notation, tablature and chords.

While it has a different focus than **Easy Ukulele**, there is some repetition of the fundamentals to ensure it can stand alone. Users of my first book can skip over certain sections, although reviewing these basics can be useful.

Consider subscribing to the **Pierre Hache Music YouTube Channel** where you'll find plenty of free video lessons that complement both books. You can take your learning to the next level with play-along tutorials, practice tips and easy versions of tricky chords.

As a teacher, my goal is to keep my students' attention and provide the tools for them to achieve tangible results. Most importantly, the process should be fun! My advice for students of all levels is simple: work on one thing at a time; don't skip the fundamentals; listen to lots of music; and when in doubt, SLOW DOWN!

Thanks and Happy Playing,

Pierre

# TABLE OF CONTENTS

## Theory and Exercises

Practice Makes Progress . . . . . . . . 1
Your Ukulele . . . . . . . . . . . . . . . . 1
How to Tune Your Ukulele . . . . . . 2
How to Hold Your Ukulele . . . . . . 4
Strings, Frets and Fingers . . . . . . . 5
Technique . . . . . . . . . . . . . . . . . . 6
Reading Notes and Tablature . . . . 7
Reading Rhythm . . . . . . . . . . . . . 9
Rhythm Exercises . . . . . . . . . . . . 10
Notes on the First String . . . . . . . 11
Notes on the Second String . . . . . 13
Notes on the Third String . . . . . . 15
Combining the Strings . . . . . . . . 17
Basic Chords . . . . . . . . . . . . . . . 19
First Songs . . . . . . . . . . . . . . . . . 22
Pickups and Ties . . . . . . . . . . . . . 28
Waltz Time . . . . . . . . . . . . . . . . 31
Eighth Notes . . . . . . . . . . . . . . . 34
More Chords . . . . . . . . . . . . . . . 37
Strumming Patterns . . . . . . . . . . 38
Chord Progressions . . . . . . . . . . 39
B Flat . . . . . . . . . . . . . . . . . . . . 43
High D . . . . . . . . . . . . . . . . . . . 53

**Thank You!** . . . . . . . . . . . . . . . 58
Also From Pierre Haché Music . . . 59

## Songs

Hot Cross Buns . . . . . . . . . . . . . 22
Are You Sleeping? . . . . . . . . . . . 23
Au Claire de la Lune . . . . . . . . . . 24
Twinkle, Twinkle Little Star . . . . . 25
Ode to Joy . . . . . . . . . . . . . . . . 26
Mary Had a Little Lamb . . . . . . . 27
London Bridge . . . . . . . . . . . . . 27
When the Saints Go Marching In . . . . . 30
Humpty Dumpty . . . . . . . . . . . . 32
For He's a Jolly Good Fellow . . . . 33
This Old Man . . . . . . . . . . . . . . 35
Baa Baa Black Sheep . . . . . . . . . 36
It's Raining, It's Pouring . . . . . . . 41
Give My Regards to Broadway . . . . . . 42
Happy Birthday . . . . . . . . . . . . . 44
Skip to My Lou . . . . . . . . . . . . . 45
Yankee Doodle . . . . . . . . . . . . . 45
The Itsy Bitsy Spider . . . . . . . . . . 46
Bingo . . . . . . . . . . . . . . . . . . . . 47
Down in the Valley . . . . . . . . . . 47
Aura Lee . . . . . . . . . . . . . . . . . . 48
If You're Happy and You Know It . . . . . 49
Hush Little Baby . . . . . . . . . . . . 50
Snake Charmer . . . . . . . . . . . . . 50
She'll be Comin' Round the Mountain . . . 51
Rockin' Robin . . . . . . . . . . . . . . 52
Sea Shanty . . . . . . . . . . . . . . . . 53
Amazing Grace . . . . . . . . . . . . . 54
Take Me Out to the Ballgame . . . . . . 55
U-kin' Blues . . . . . . . . . . . . . . . . 57

# PRACTICE MAKES PROGRESS

The key to unlocking the JOY in music is regular practice. To get started, three or four times a week for 15 minutes is plenty. I suggest keeping your ukulele and books somewhere accessible, inviting, comfortable and well lit.

Note that these pages are designed to be practiced in order. Take your time, progress at your own pace and enjoy your musical journey!

# YOUR UKULELE

The soprano is the smallest ukulele, followed by the concert and tenor. The exercises and songs in this book will work perfectly with each of these sizes, as long as your instrument is tuned to a standard **C** tuning, as outlined in the next section.

The following diagram shows the different parts of your ukulele.

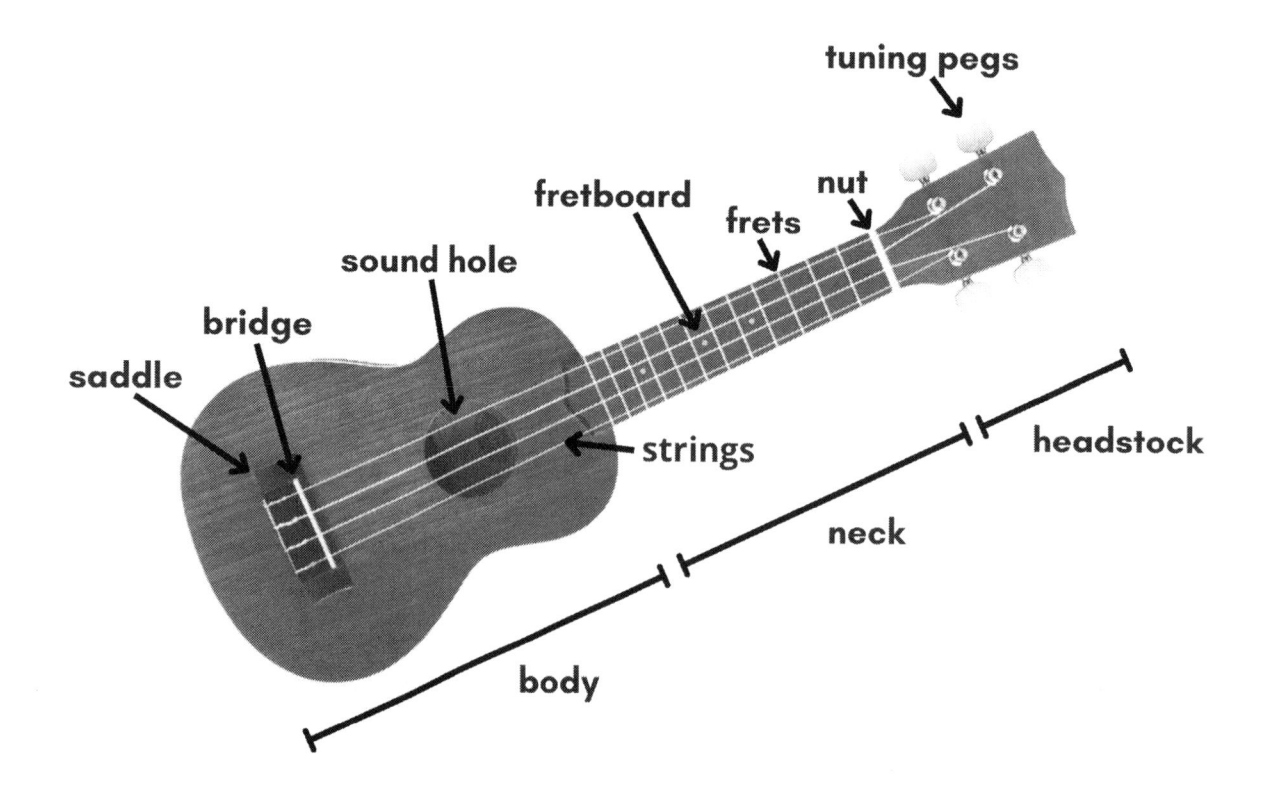

# HOW TO TUNE YOUR UKULELE

An important first step to making your ukulele sound beautiful is to tune it. The easiest way is to use an electronic tuner or a tuning app.

To tune with an electronic tuner, simply attach it to the head of your ukulele or hold it near the sound hole, and pluck one string at a time. Turn the connected peg until the tuner shows the right note. Tightening the strings will raise the pitch, while loosening them will lower it. A new ukulele will often require many turns and regular tuning for the first week or so.

For a standard **C** tuning, the **4th** string (top) should be a **G,** the **3rd** string a **C,** the **2nd** an **E**, and finally the **1st** string (bottom) should be an **A**.

A great phrase to remember the string names from top to bottom is:
**G**ood **C**hildren **E**at **A**pples.

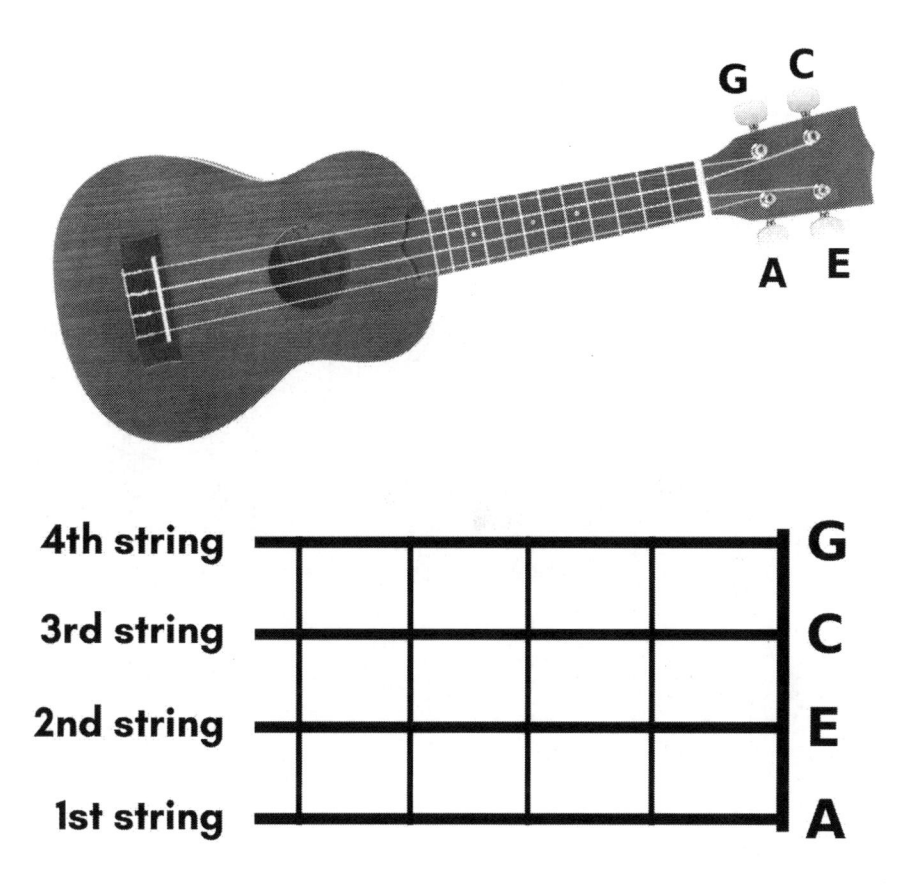

You can also tune by ear using another instrument such as a piano, a video or an app that plays the desired notes.

Simply play a **G** on the instrument and match the pitch on your **G** string by turning the corresponding peg. Or, listen to the video and match the pitches, making sure you're tuning each string to the right note. This method works best for someone with a good ear or some musical training.

# HOW TO HOLD YOUR UKULELE

If you're right-handed, hold the main body of the ukulele by pressing it against your body with your right forearm. Your hand should be near the sound hole. (see pictures below) This may be a little awkward at first, but the idea is to support, pluck and strum the instrument all with your right arm.

You can strum with your thumb, the nail of your index, or a pick; whichever feels most comfortable to you. There are felt, leather and rubber picks especially made for ukuleles, but softer guitar picks also work well.

Your other hand supports the neck and presses on the strings to change the notes.

You can play either sitting on a solid chair or standing. Keep your back straight. A music stand or something to hold your books and sheet music near eye level will help with your posture and concentration.

For left-handed players simply switch it around: hold the ukulele against your body with your left arm, while the right hand supports the neck and presses the strings.

**How to hold your ukulele**

**Strum with your thumb**    **The nail of your index**    **Or a pick**

# STRINGS, FRETS AND FINGERS

As we saw in the tuning section, the strings of your ukulele are numbered **4 3 2 1** from top to bottom, and when tuned, sound the notes **G C E A**. (**G**ood **C**hildren **E**at **A**pples)

The frets are numbered **1, 2, 3** and so on, starting with the one closest to the headstock.

We'll also number the fingers of your pressing hand, **1, 2, 3** and **4**, starting with your index finger.

Take a minute to study the diagrams below.

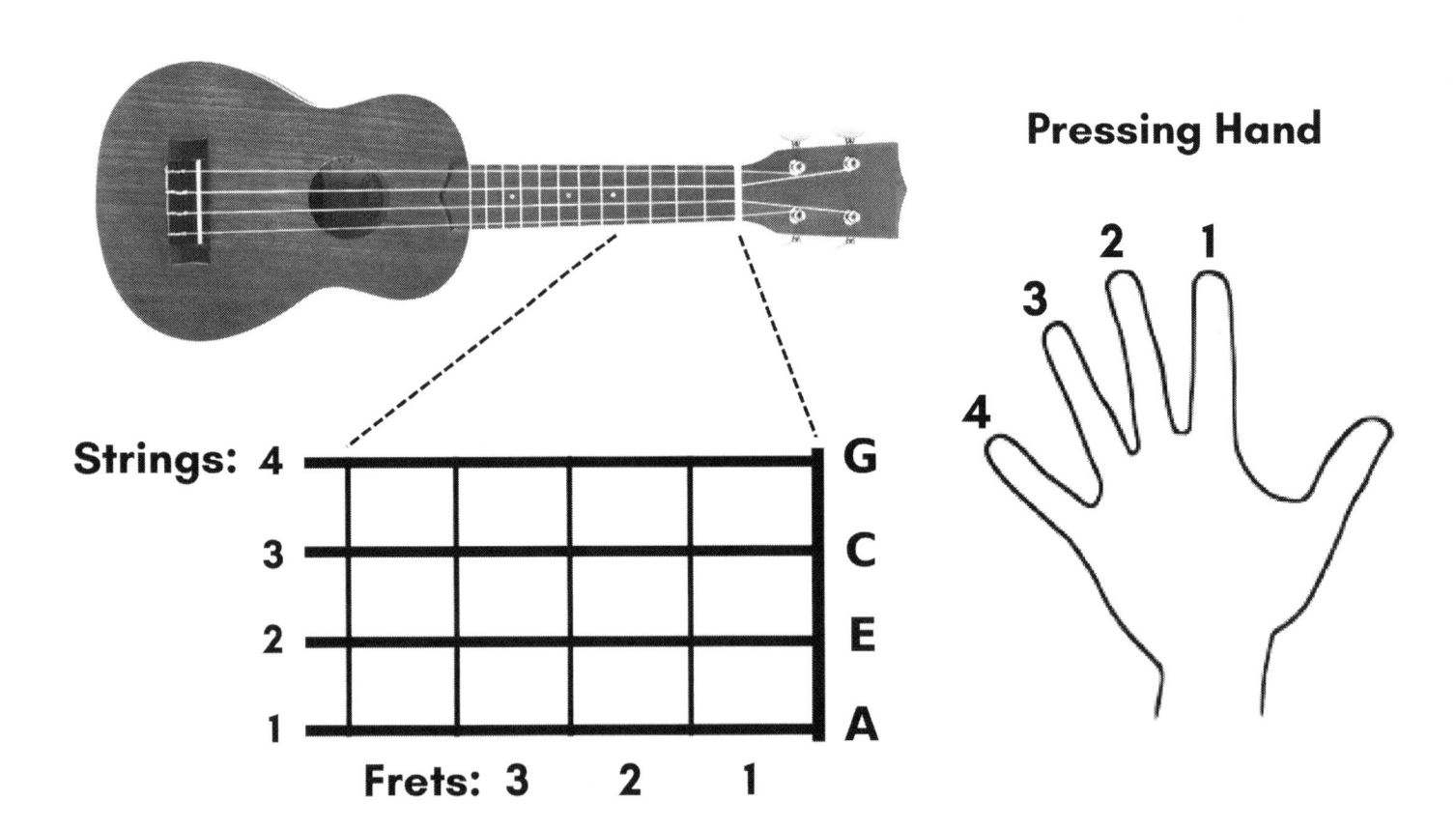

# TECHNIQUE

The following are a few important notes on proper technique:

- Keep the thumb of your pressing hand behind the neck.

- Press with the very tips of your fingers to avoid touching and muting other strings.

- Press firmly between the metal bars, or frets, on the side nearest the body of your ukulele. This makes it easier to produce clear ringing notes.

- Don't hold the ukulele with the fingers of your plucking hand. You want to keep it free for plucking and strumming. Your hand should float near the sound hole while your forearm hugs the instrument against your body. Some players like to use a strap to provide additional support.

**Thumb behind the neck**

**Tips of fingers between the frets**

**Don't hold the ukulele with the fingers of your plucking hand**

**Float your hand near the sound hole supporting the ukulele with your forearm**

# READING NOTES AND TABLATURE

There are two types of notation in this book: musical notation in a staff and tablature, or TAB.

A staff is a group of five lines with four spaces. These do *not* represent the strings of your ukulele; rather each line and space represents a pitch, or how low or high a note is. The lowest note is **middle C**, which is on an extra line (or ledger line) below the staff. To the left of the staff is a clef sign. Ukulele music is always written in treble clef.

The vertical lines that divide the notes are called bar lines. They divide the music into rhythmic groups called bars, or measures. In this book, songs have three or four beats per measure.

The **4/4** to the left is called a time signature. **4/4** means 4 quarter notes, or beats per measure, whereas **3/4** means 3 beats per measure.

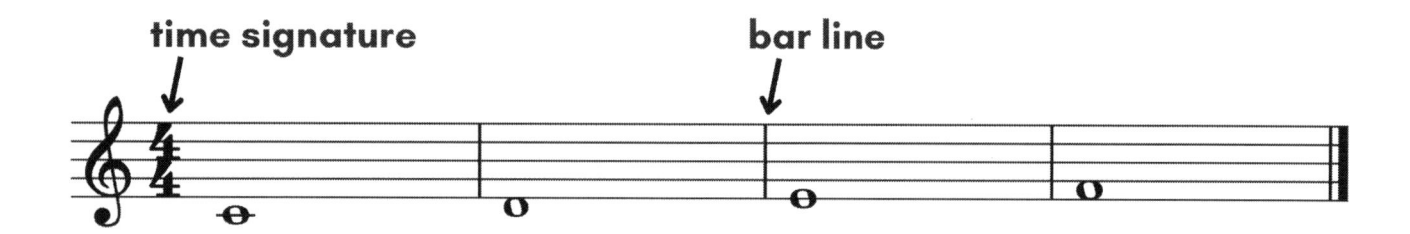

Each line and space of the musical staff has a note name. The **spaces** spell **F A C E** from bottom to top. The **lines**, from bottom to top, can be remembered with the phrase **E**very **G**ood **B**oy **D**eserves **F**udge.

Unlike musical notation, the four lines of tablature *do* represent the strings of your ukulele. The bottom line is your **4th**, or top string. The numbers in the TAB tell you what fret to press. The line on which the number is placed tells you what string to press and pluck.

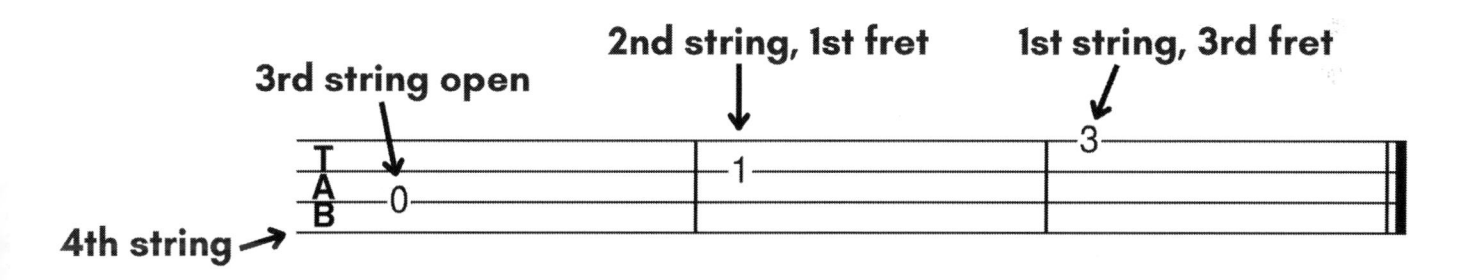

The advantage of traditional musical notation is that it is transferable to other instruments and tells you the exact rhythmic value of each note. TAB can be a great tool for learning, but can also become a crutch. Some of the songs and exercises in this book won't include TAB to help you learn the notes in the staff.

# READING RHYTHM

Rhythm is just as important as notes when it comes to reading music. We'll start by learning three basic rhythms: **whole notes**, **half notes** and **quarter notes**. Each one lasts a different number of beats.

Start by counting to 4 at a slow and steady pace with no pauses:
**1, 2, 3, 4, 1, 2, 3, 4, 1 . . .**

**Whole notes** ( o ) last four beats, or a whole measure. Let's play them as an **A** by plucking the **1st** string. Let the string ring as you continue to count. Make sure the note sounds exactly as you say **1**, not before or after.

Continue counting, and pluck every time you say **1**.

| o | o | o | o |
|---|---|---|---|
| 1  2  3  4 | 1  2  3  4 | 1  2  3  4 | 1  2  3  4 |

Congratulations, you're playing whole notes!

**Half notes** ( ♩ ) last two beats. To play half notes, pluck the **A** string when you say **1** and **3**. Keep your count steady, and let the notes ring for two full beats.

| 1  2  3  4 | 1  2  3  4 | 1  2  3  4 | 1  2  3  4 |
|---|---|---|---|

**Quarter notes** ( ♩ ) last one beat. To play quarter notes, pluck on every count.

| 1  2  3  4 | 1  2  3  4 | 1  2  3  4 | 1  2  3  4 |
|---|---|---|---|

# RHYTHM EXERCISES

Play the following reading exercises slowly while counting out loud. Pluck the **1st** string, or an **A** note. Make sure to let the notes ring and keep your count steady. You can also try these rhythms on different strings.

Choose the plucking method that works best for you, and remember not to hold the ukulele with the fingers of your plucking hand.

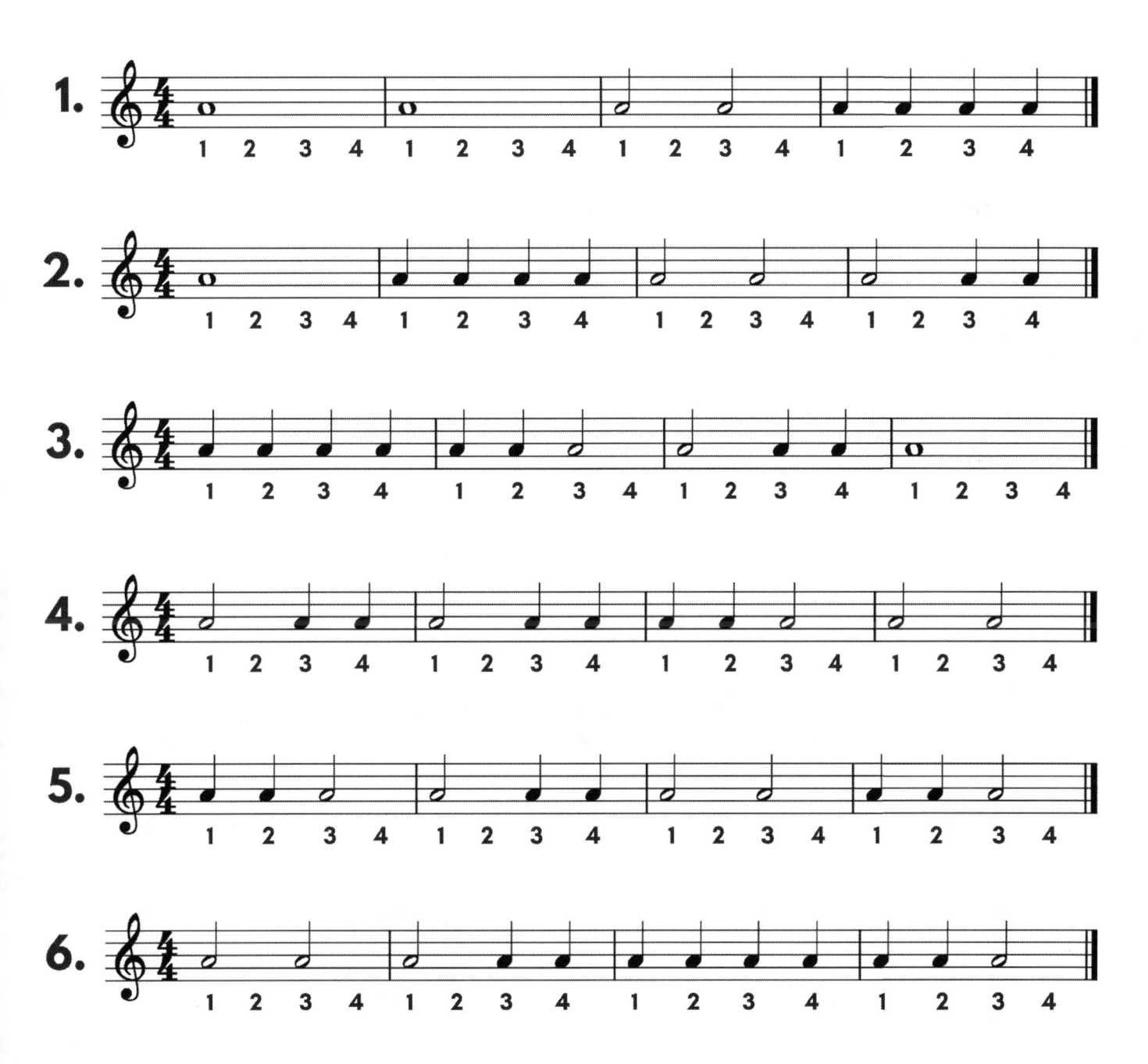

# NOTES ON THE FIRST STRING

As we saw in the previous sections, the **1st** string open is an **A**.
Here, we see that the **2nd** fret is a **B**, and the **3rd** fret, a **C**.

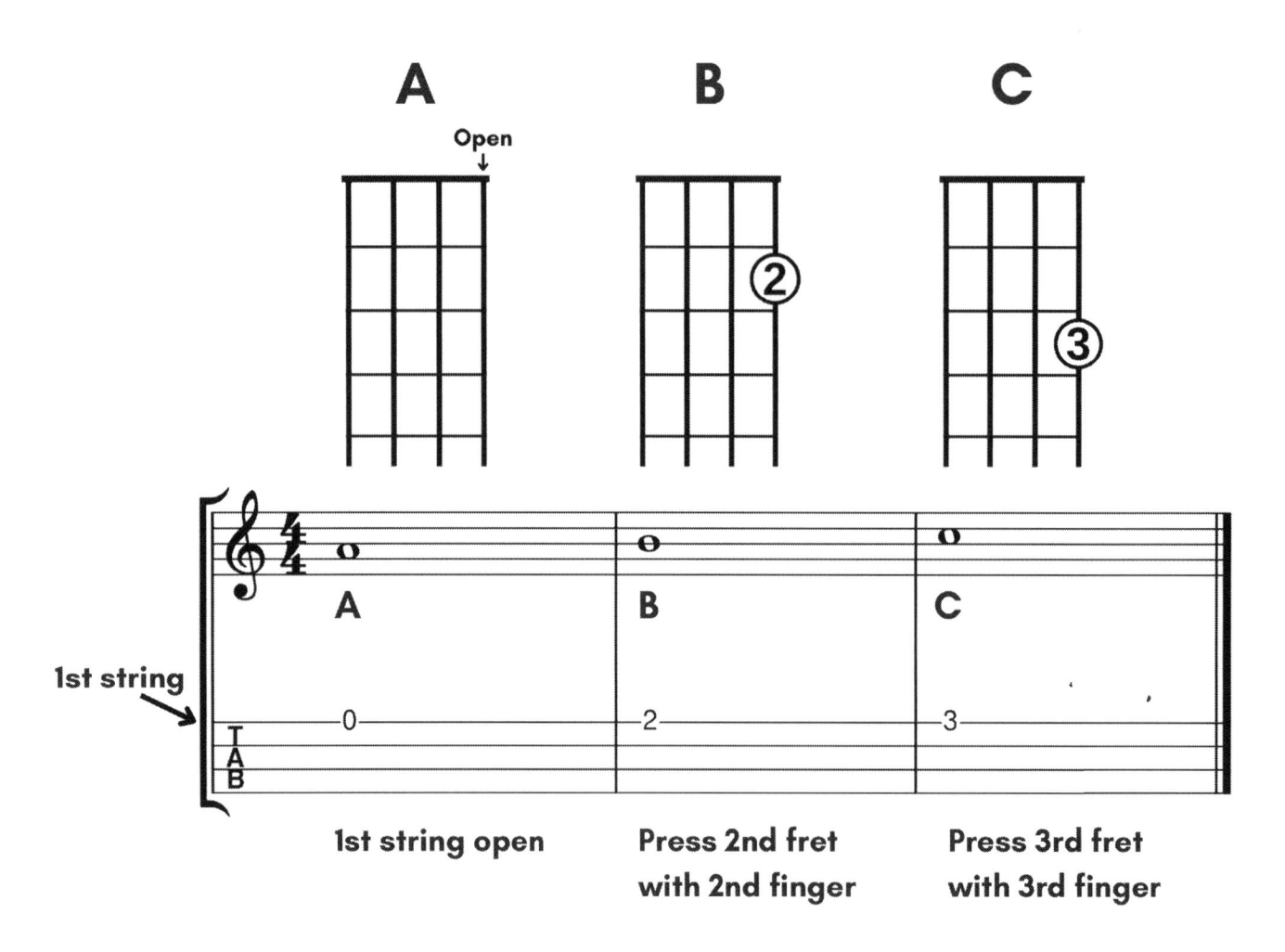

**A** — 1st string open

**B** — Press 2nd fret with 2nd finger

**C** — Press 3rd fret with 3rd finger

Name the notes in the following exercise. Then, play it slowly.
For an added challenge, **count out loud** or **hum along** as you pluck.

First name the notes, then play the following exercises. Remember half notes last two beats and quarter notes last one. Refer to the previous page as needed.

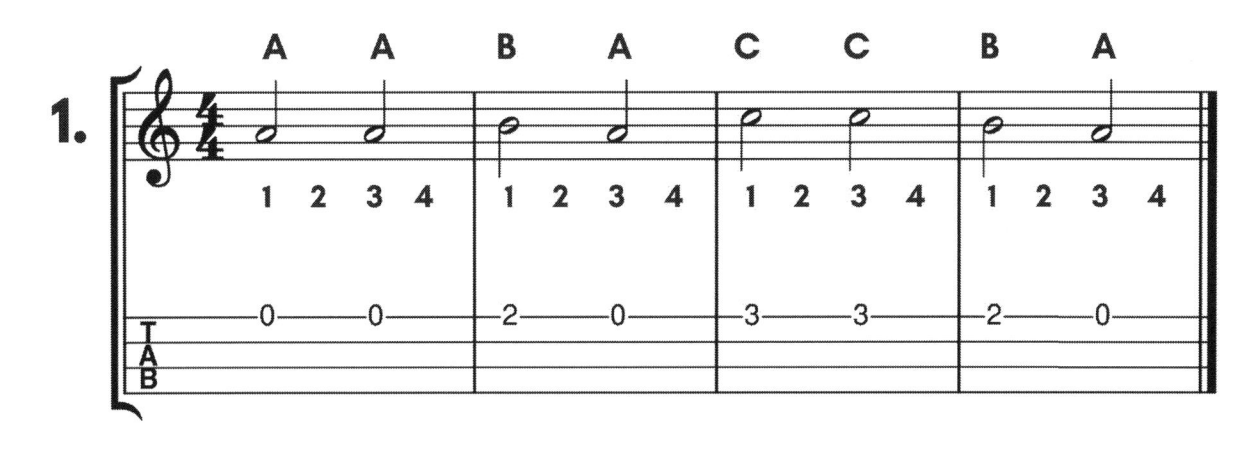

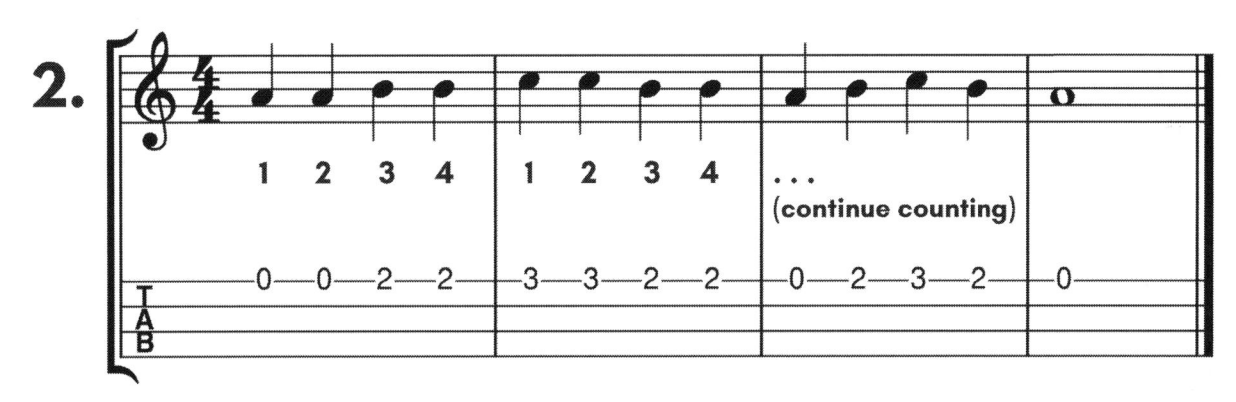

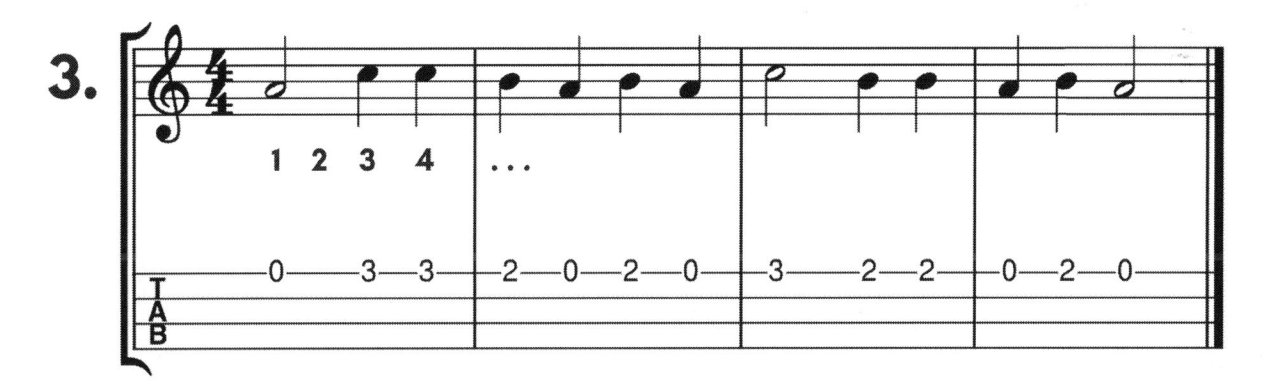

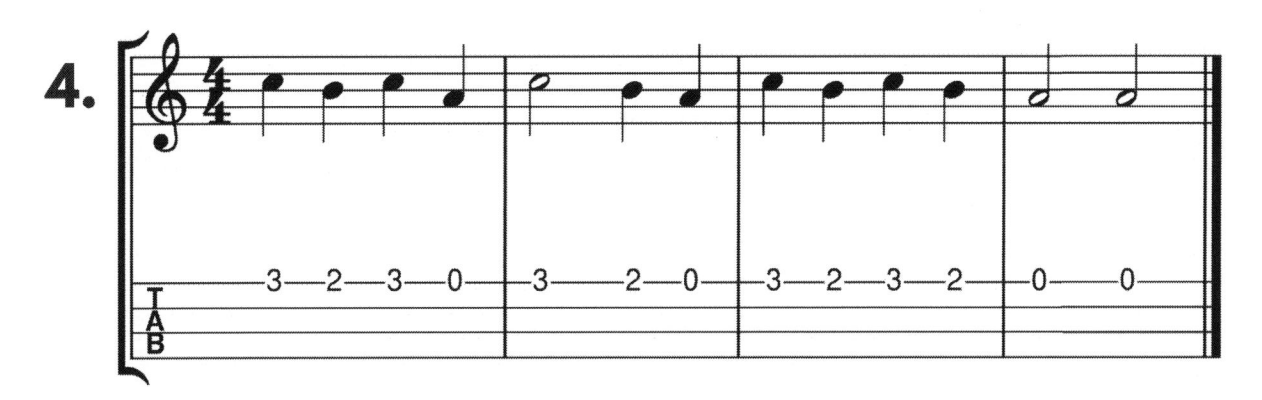

# NOTES ON THE SECOND STRING

The **2nd** string open is an **E**. The **1st** fret is an **F**, and the **3rd** fret, a **G**.

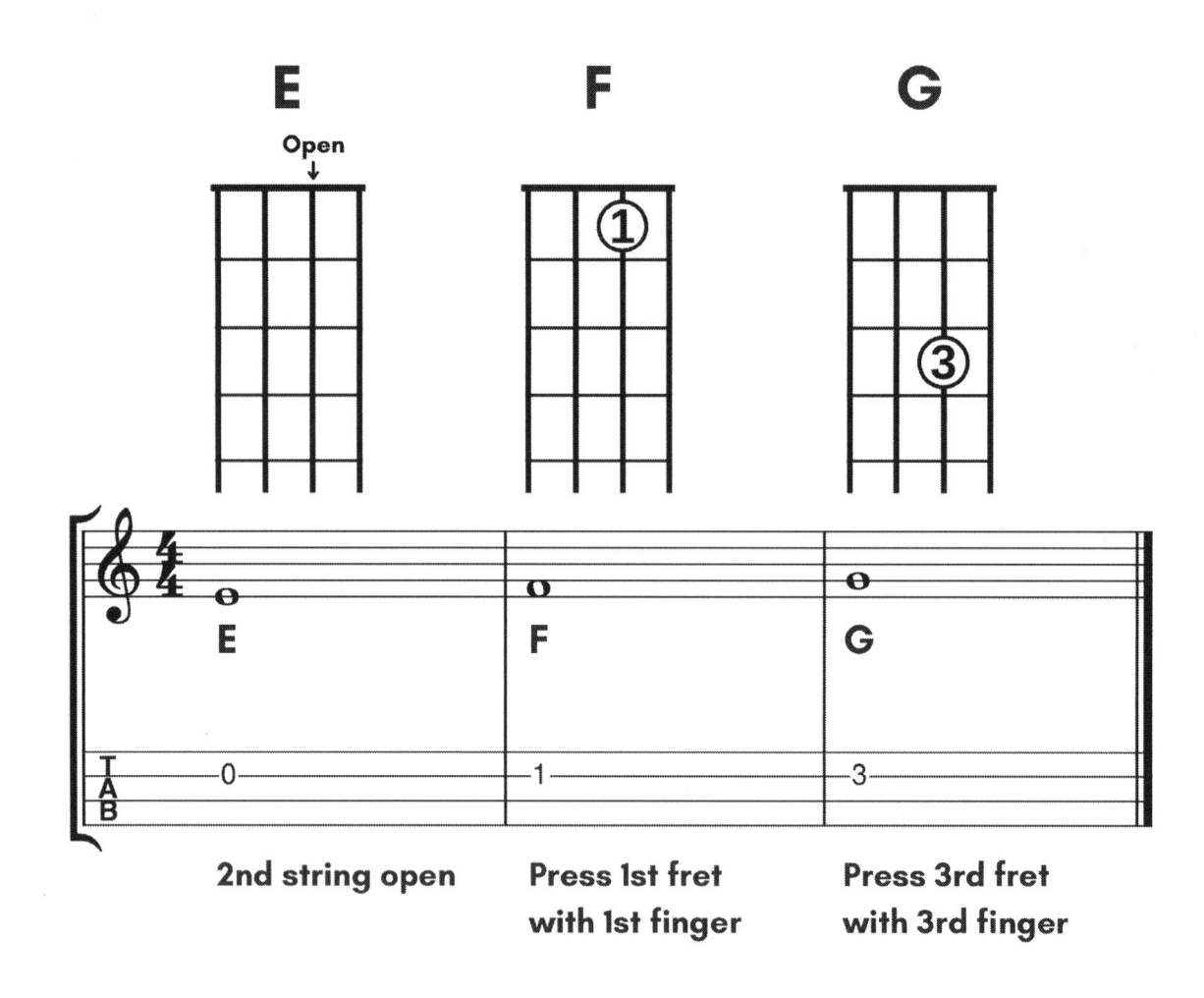

**E** — Open
**F** — ①
**G** — ③

2nd string open
Press 1st fret with 1st finger
Press 3rd fret with 3rd finger

Name the notes in the following exercise. Then, play it slowly.
For an added challenge, **count out loud** or **hum along** as you pluck.

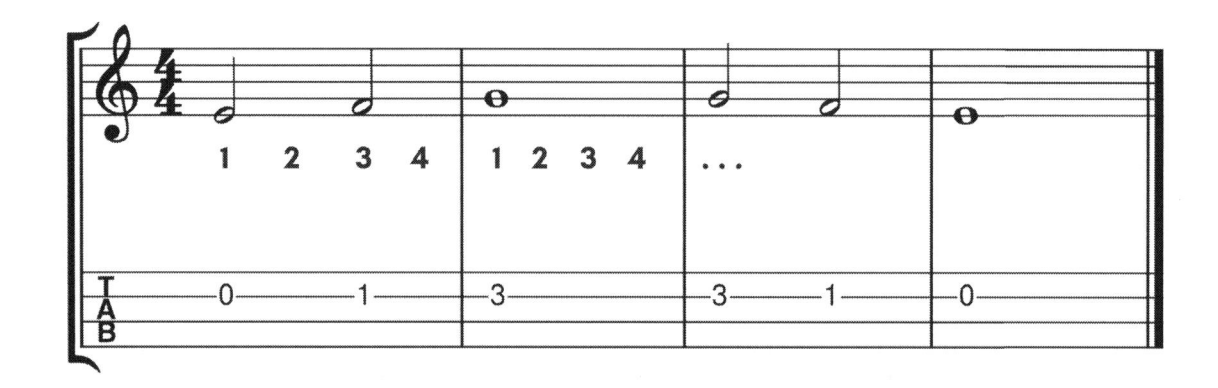

1 2 3 4 | 1 2 3 4 | . . . |

TAB: 0 — 1 | 3 | 3 — 1 | 0

13

First name the notes, then play the following exercises.

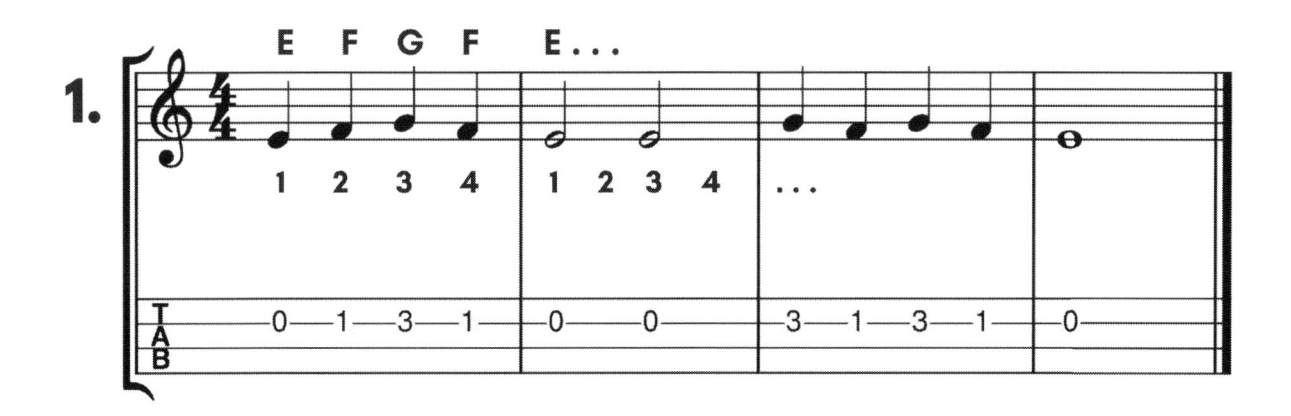

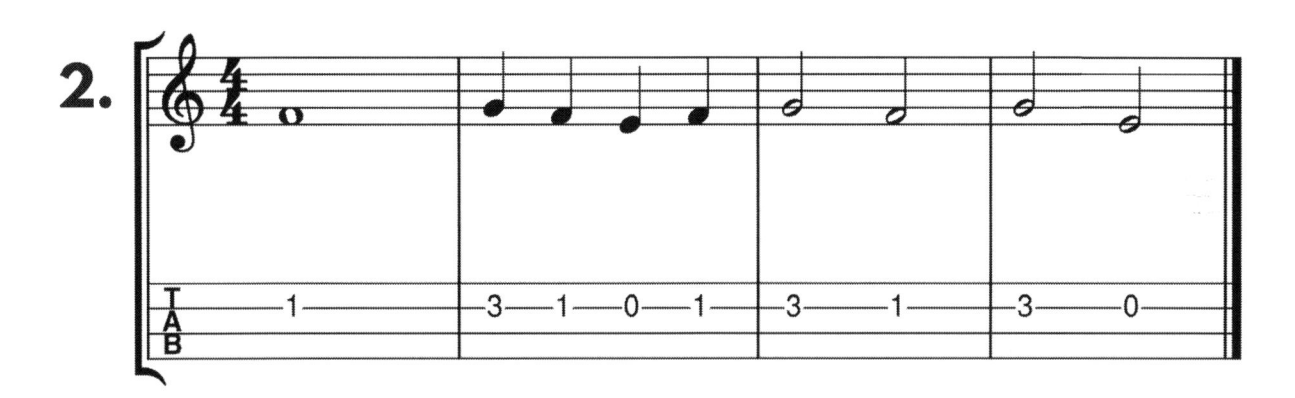

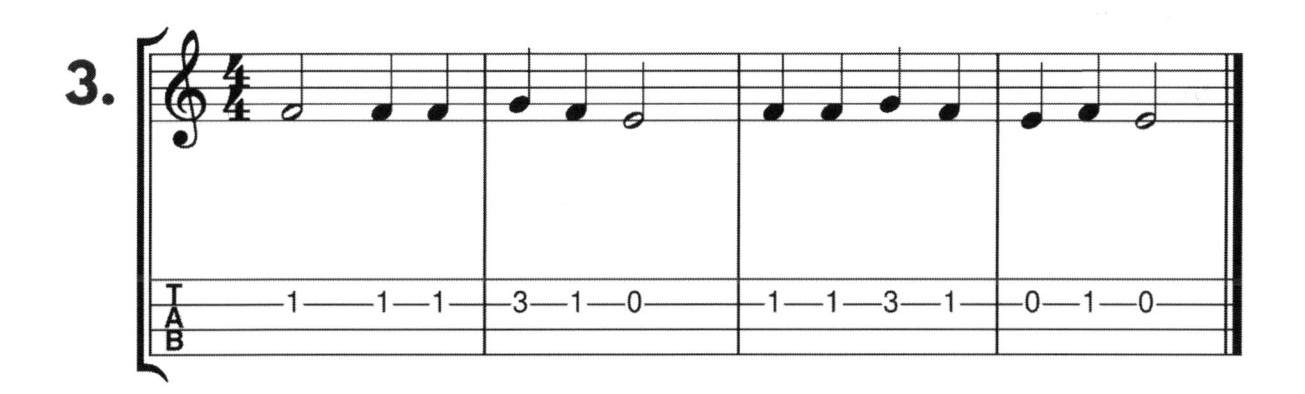

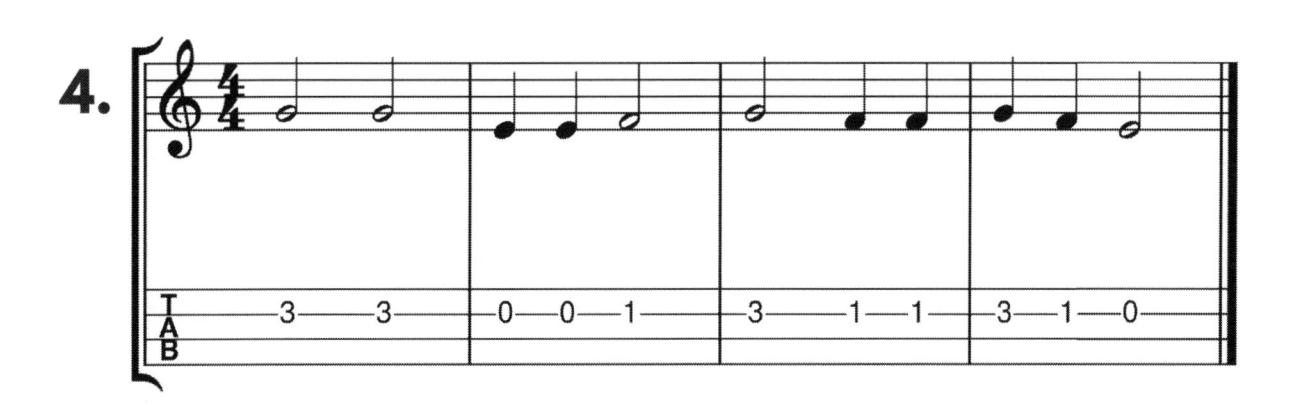

# NOTES ON THE THIRD STRING

The **3rd** string open is a **C**. The **2nd** fret is a **D**.

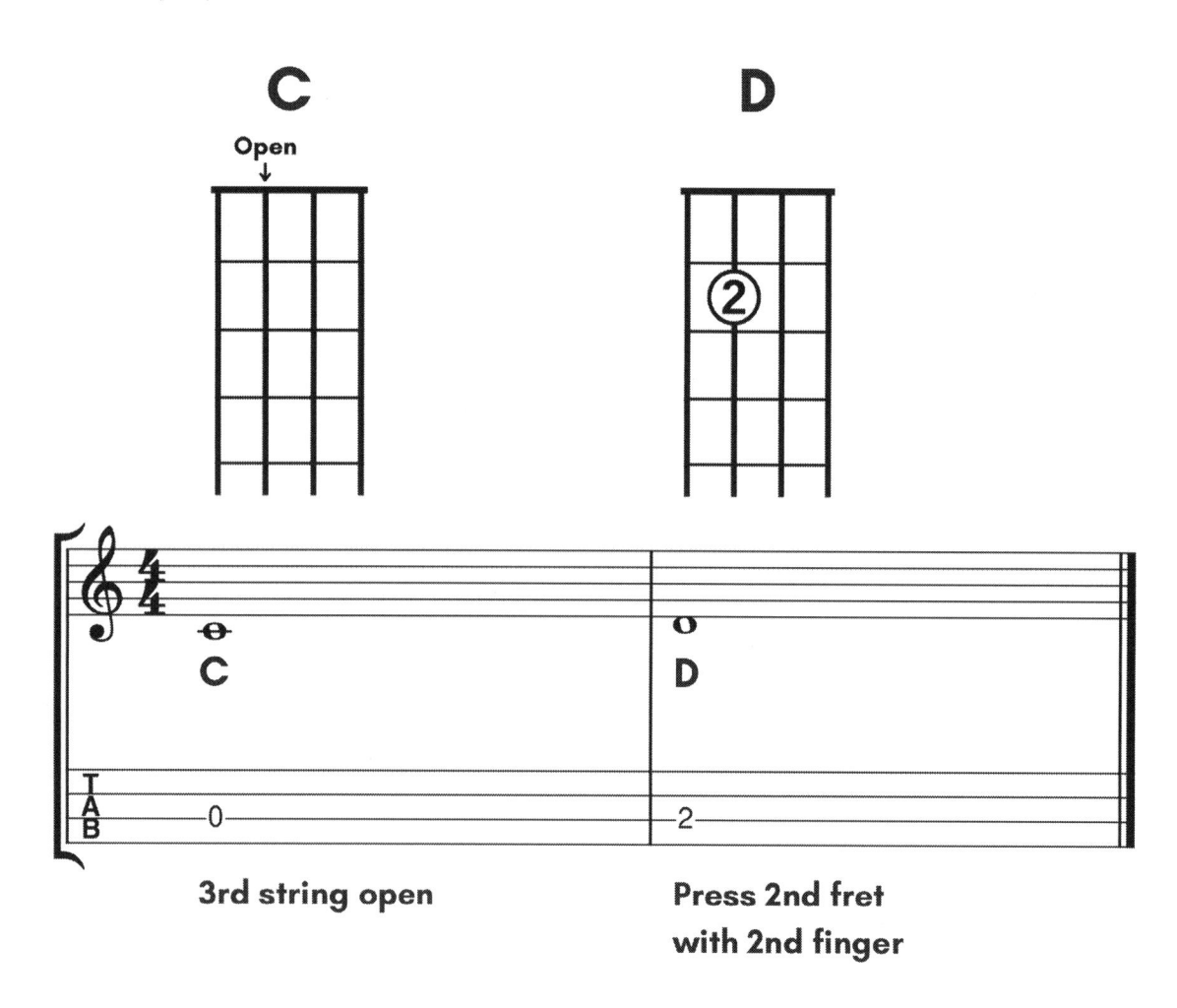

**3rd string open**

**Press 2nd fret with 2nd finger**

Name the notes in the following exercise. Then, play it slowly.
For an added challenge, **count out loud** or **hum along** as you pluck.

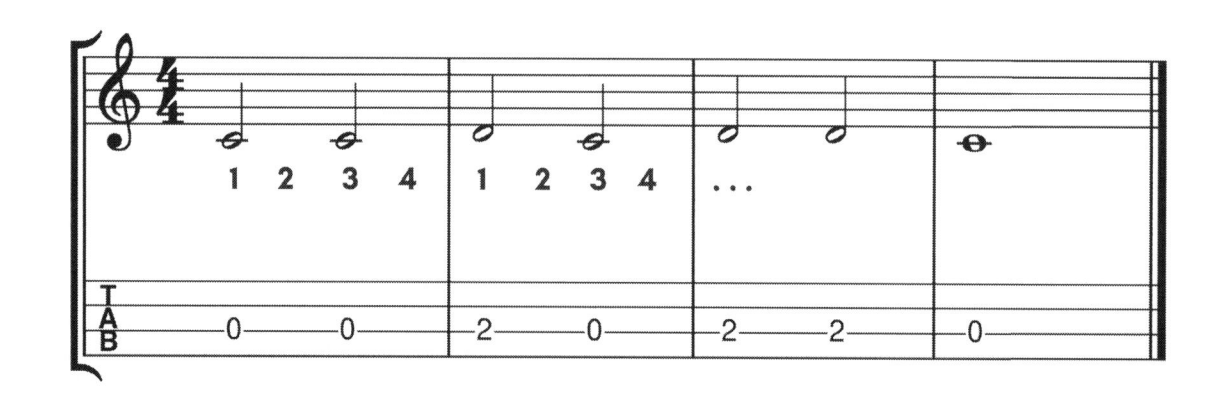

First name the notes, then play the following exercises.

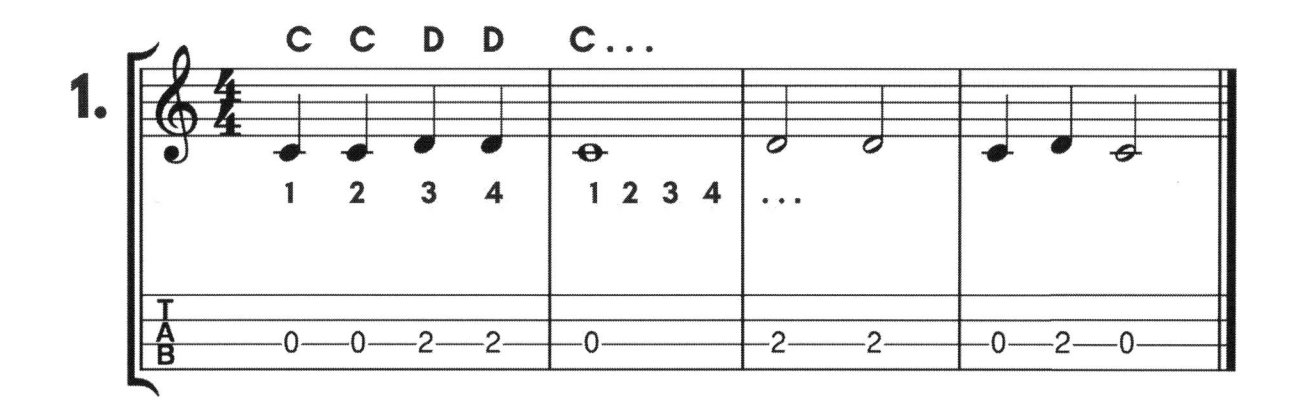

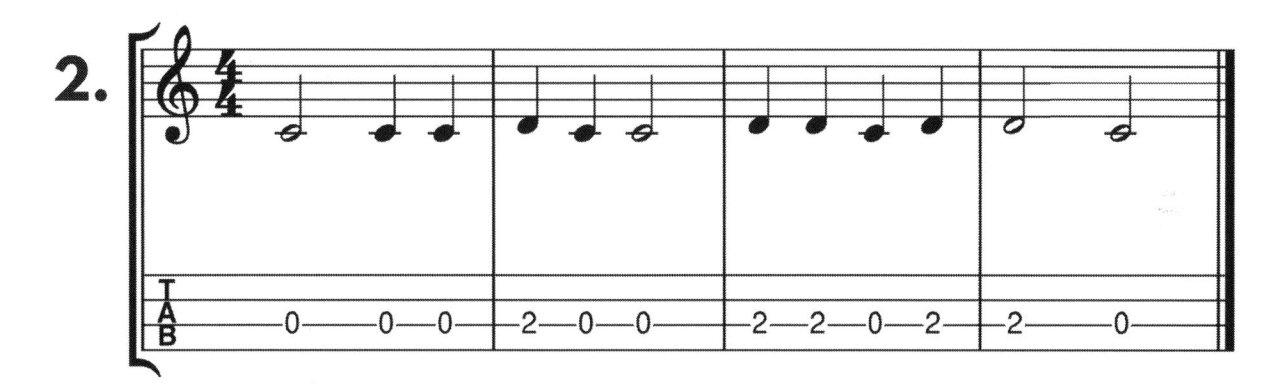

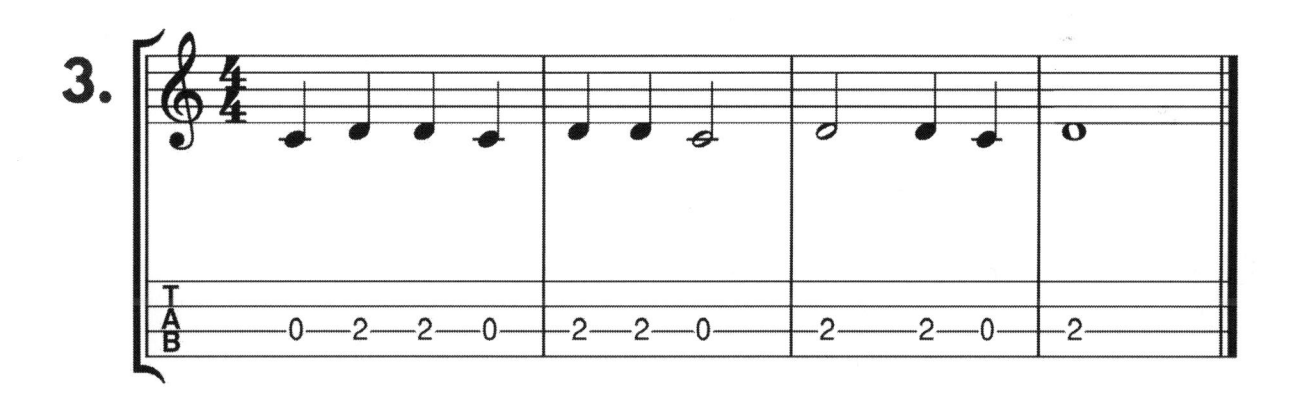

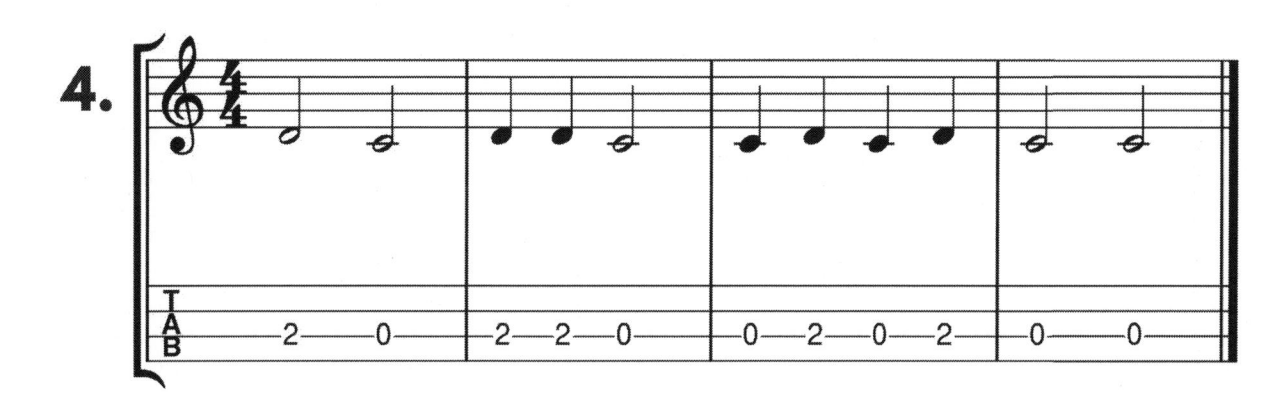

# COMBINING THE STRINGS

All the notes you've learnt so far come together to make a **C Major Scale.**

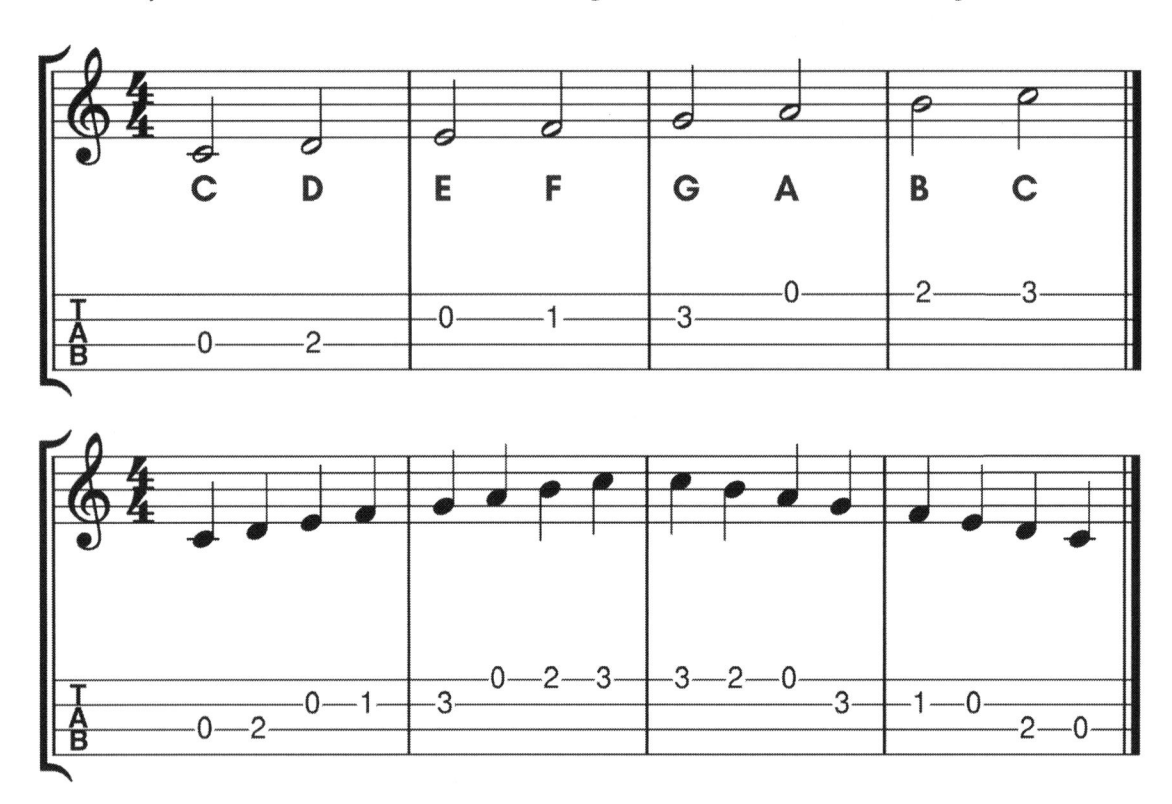

The following exercises combine the **2nd** and **3rd** strings.

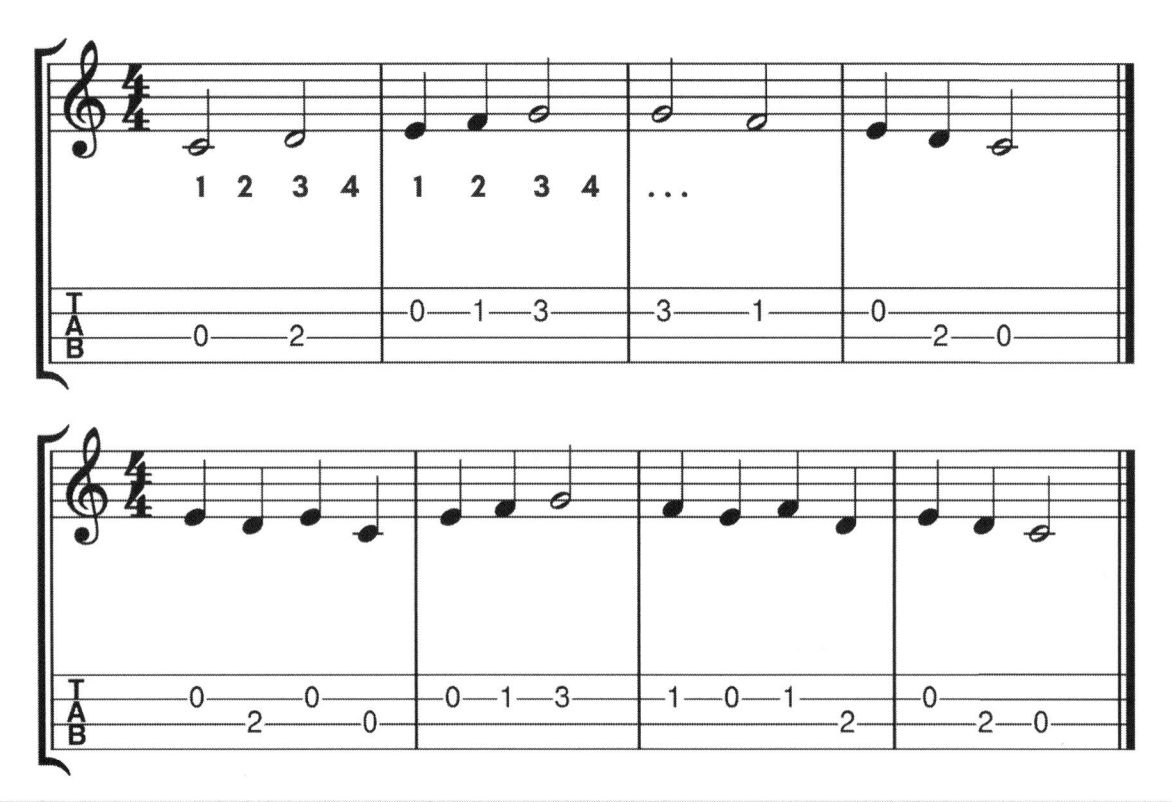

The following exercises combine the **1st** and **2nd** strings.

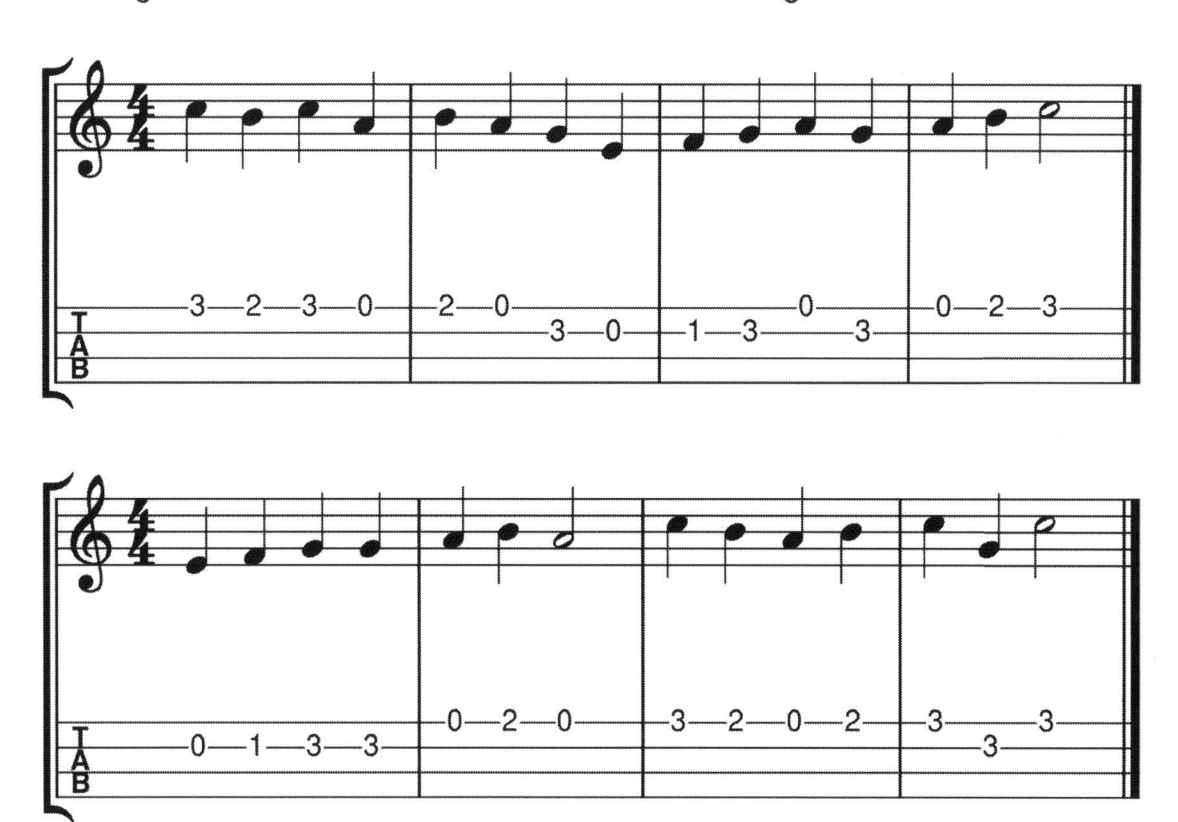

The following exercises combine all the strings. **Name**, **play** and **hum along!**

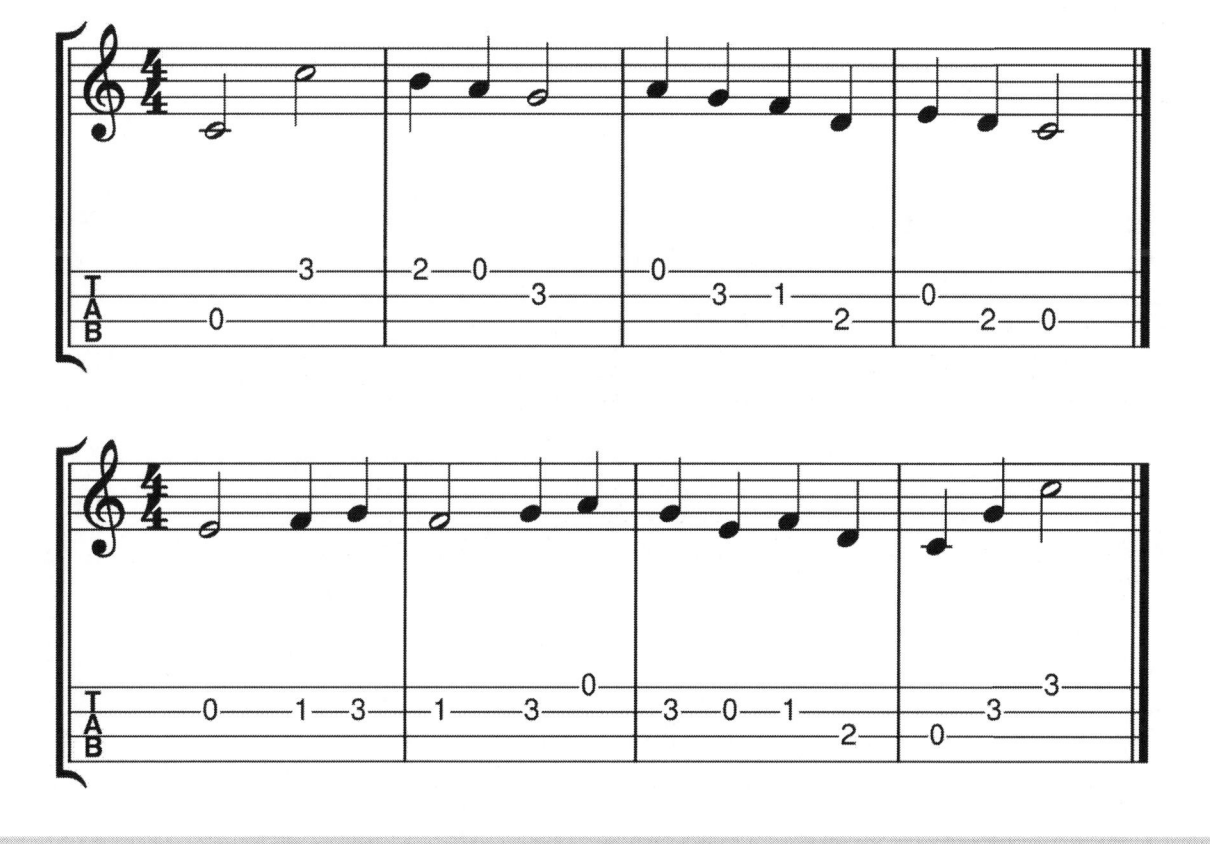

# BASIC CHORDS

Chord diagrams show you where to press on the fretboard to play a certain chord. They typically represent a vertically oriented fretboard, like a ukulele hanging on a wall.

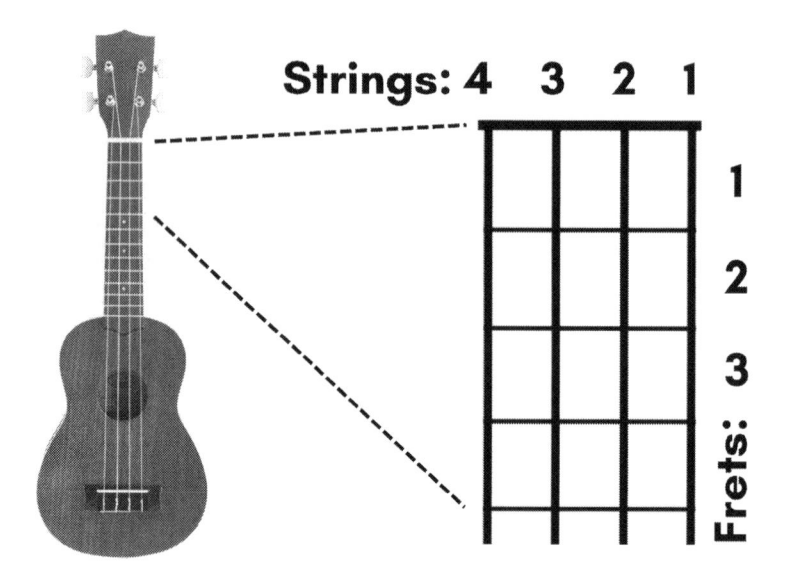

A number on a string in a chord diagram tells you which finger to use. Here are some examples.

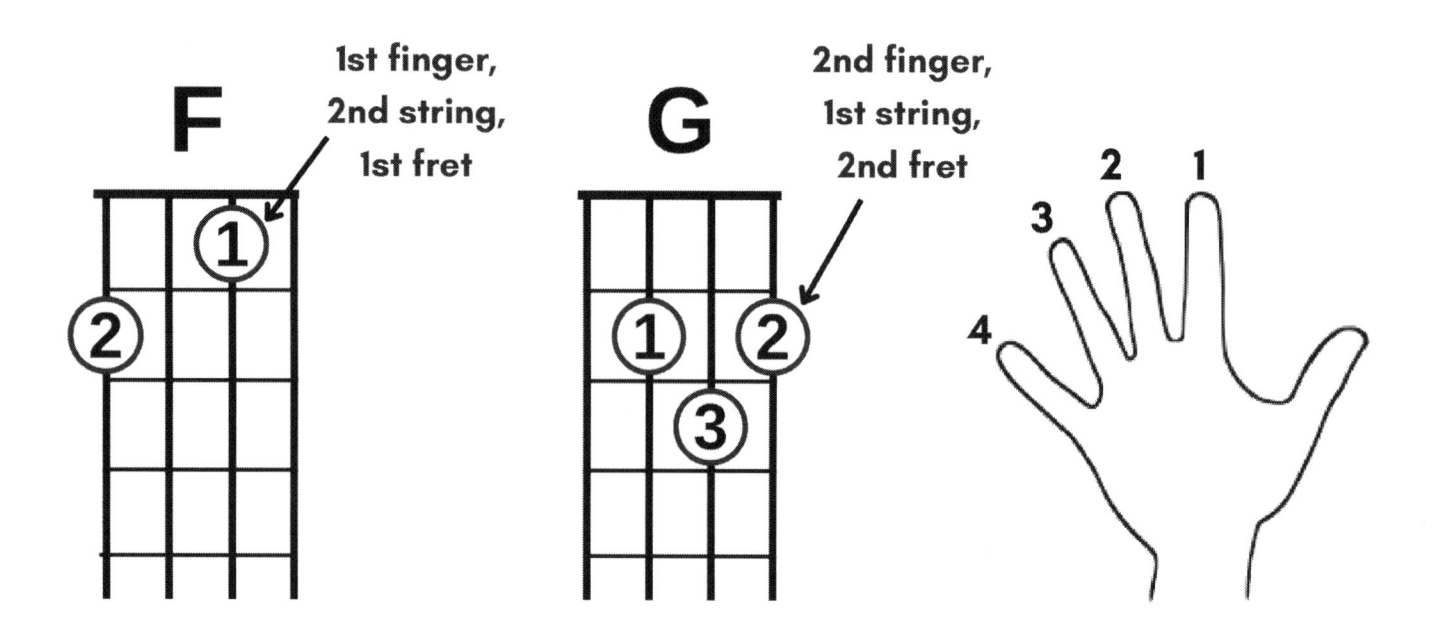

19

Before we dive into playing songs, let's learn some chords.

The following are some of the most common ukulele chords. The **F** and **G** may take some time to get used to, so be patient. Keep your thumb behind the neck, and press with the very tips of your fingers to avoid muting any strings. Gently strum all 4 strings downwards with your thumb, the nail of your index finger or a soft pick. The goal is to get a clear, ringing sound with each string.

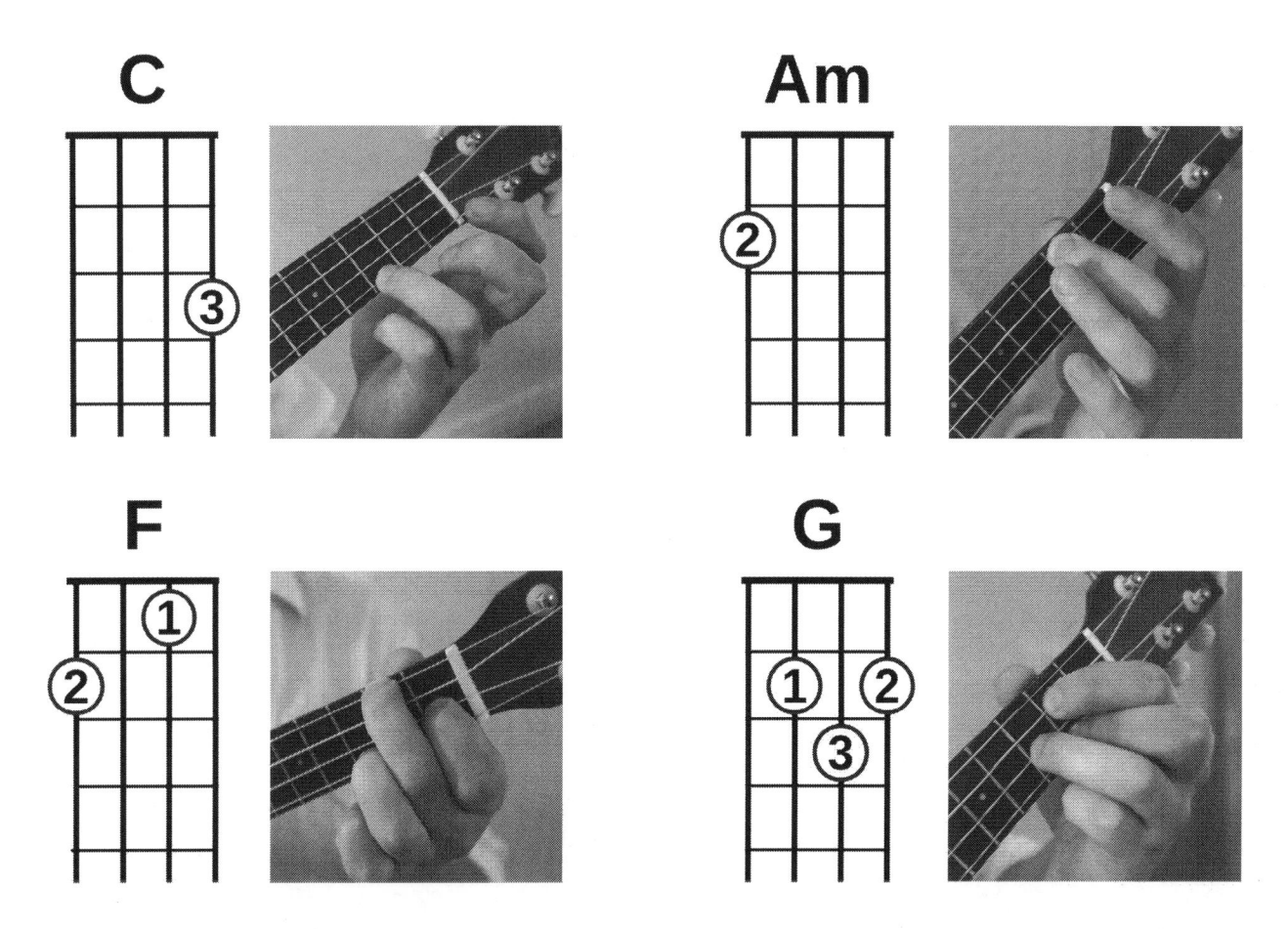

## C

## Am

## F

## G

Once you can get a nice sound, the next step is to work on **chord transitions**. Switch back and forth between the following chords 10 times. Aim for smooth, efficient movements. Start slowly – speed will come with regular practice.

C - Am - C - Am . . .

Am - F - Am - F . . .

C - F - C - F . . .

C - G - C - G . . .

Am - G - Am - G . . .

F - G - F - G . . .

It's important to play chords in "time," or with a beat. Let's start by strumming whole notes. Count to 4 out loud like we did for the rhythm exercises. Strum on every **1**, while keeping your count steady. Change chords during beats **3** and **4**. Repeat the following exercises until they sound musical and steady.

**1.**  Am              C              Am              C
      1  2  3  4   1  2  3  4   1  2  3  4   1  2  3  4

**2.**  Am              F              C              G
      1  2  3  4   1  2  3  4   1  2  3  4   1  2  3  4

To play half notes, strum on **1** and **3**. Change chords on beat **4**.

**3.**  C       C       F       F       C       C       F       F
      1  2  3  4   1  2  3  4   1  2  3  4   1  2  3  4

**4.**  Am      Am      G       G       F       F       C       C
      1  2  3  4   1  2  3  4   1  2  3  4   1  2  3  4

To play quarter notes, strum on every beat, and change quickly after beat **4**. There should be no extra pause when you change, so **start slowly!**

**5.**  C  C  C  C  G  G  G  G  C  C  C  C  F  F  F  F
      1  2  3  4  1  2  3  4  1  2  3  4  1  2  3  4

**6.**  Am Am Am Am C  C  C  C  G  G  G  G  F  F  F  F
      1  2  3  4  1  2  3  4  1  2  3  4  1  2  3  4

Great job!

Now you're ready to play some melodies, and even sing along while you strum!

# FIRST SONGS

Refer to the note summaries and chord diagrams to play the following songs. To help you learn the notes, some songs don't include the TAB. Remember, quarter notes last one beat, half notes last two and whole notes last four.

If you're having trouble remembering the notes, review pages 7 to 18.
Once you can play these melodies correctly, **try singing along.**

Finally, **sing them while strumming the chords written above the staff.**

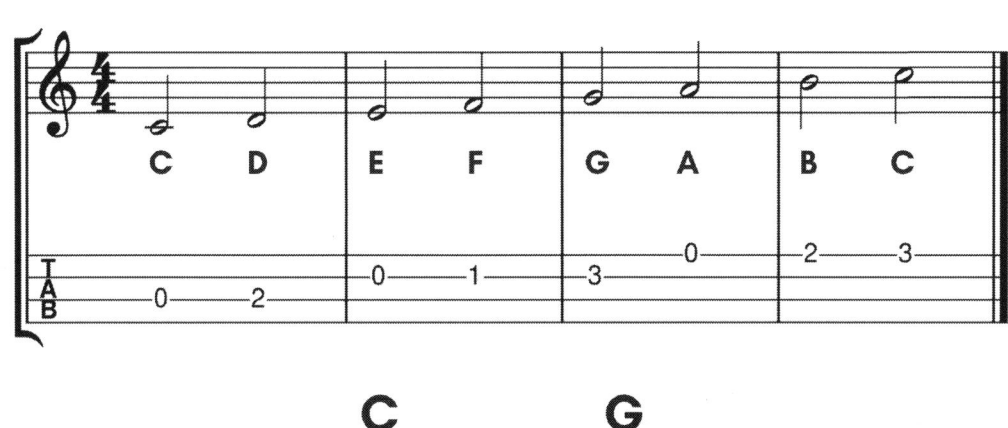

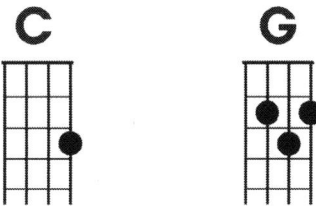

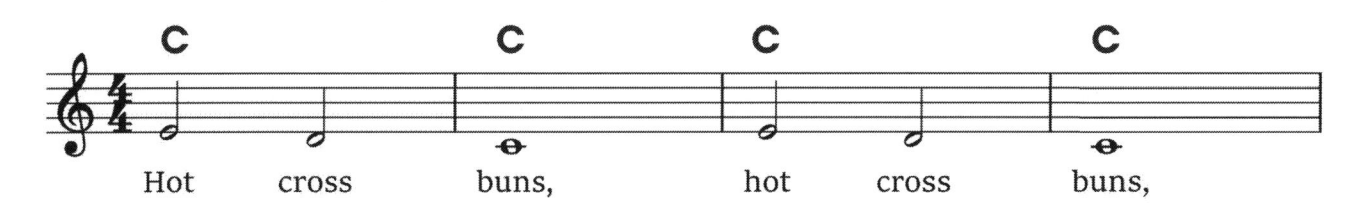

## Hot Cross Buns

Hot cross buns, hot cross buns,

One a pen-ny, two a pen-ny, hot cross buns!

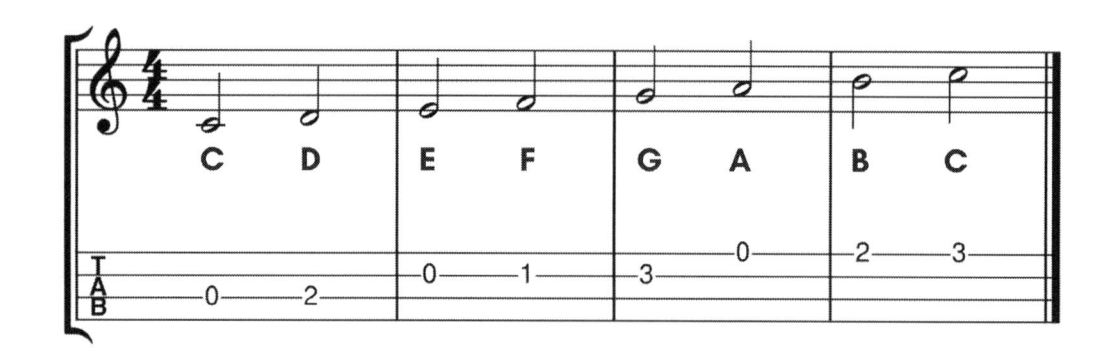

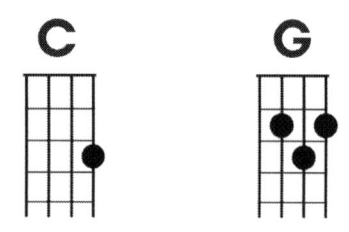

## Are You Sleeping?

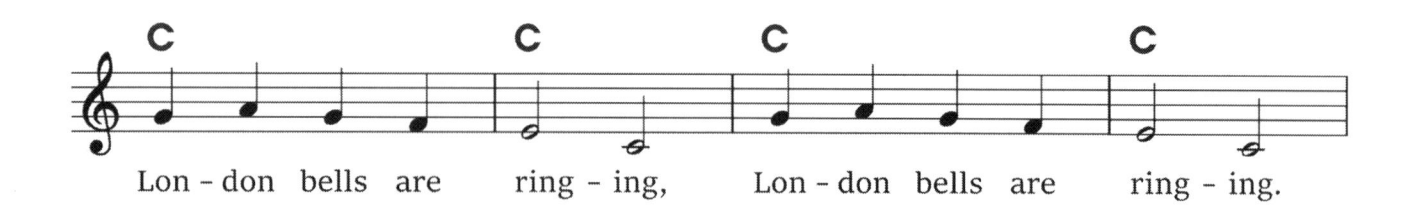

Are you sleep-ing? Are you sleep-ing?
Bro-ther John, Bro-ther John.
Lon-don bells are ring-ing, Lon-don bells are ring-ing.
Ding, dang, dong! Ding, dang, dong!

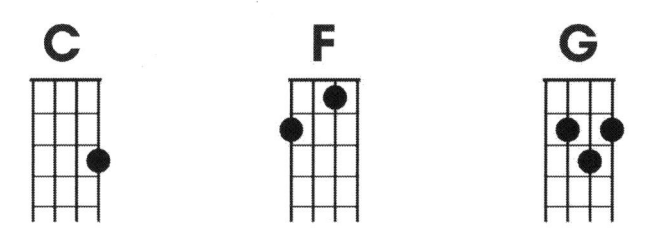

## Au Claire de la Lune

Au claire de la lune, mon a-mi Pier-rot,

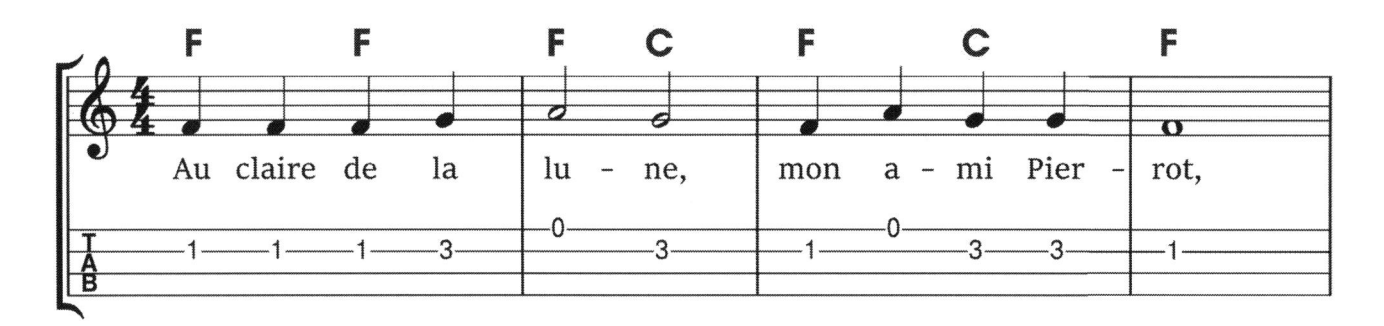

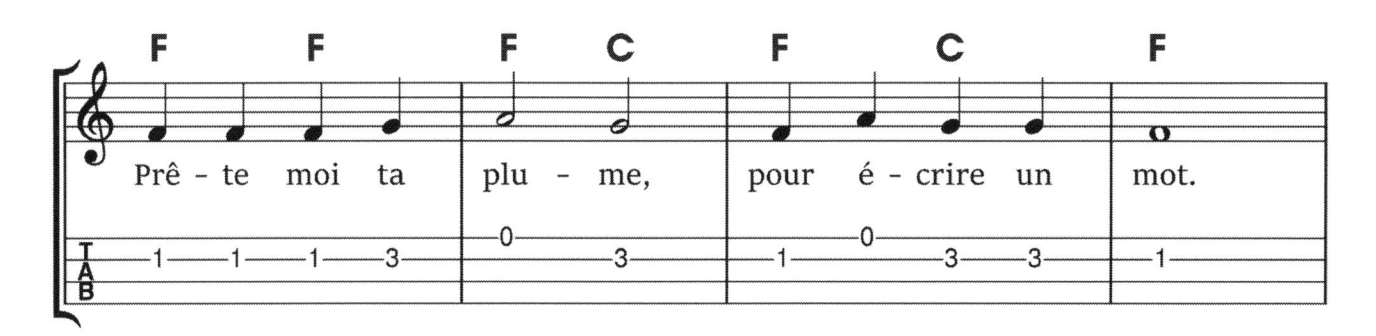

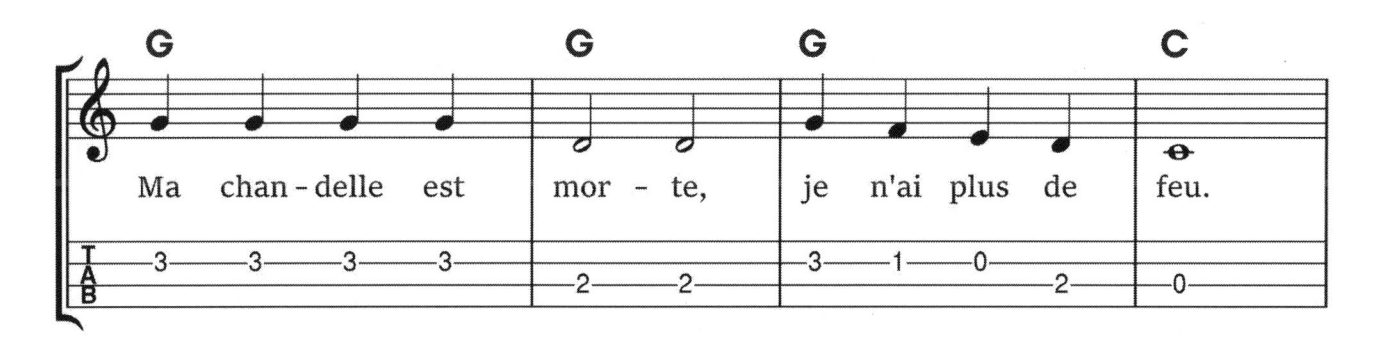

Prê-te moi ta plu-me, pour é-crire un mot.

Ma chan-delle est mor-te, je n'ai plus de feu.

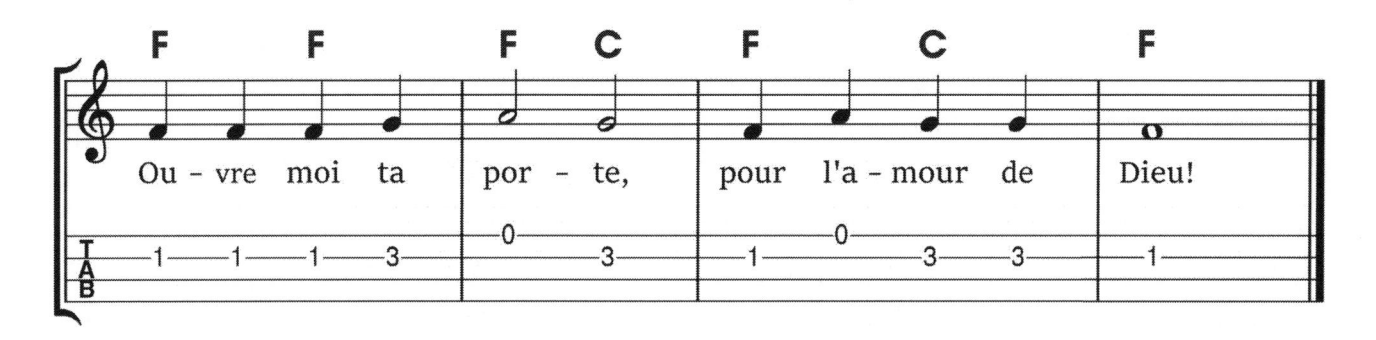

Ou-vre moi ta por-te, pour l'a-mour de Dieu!

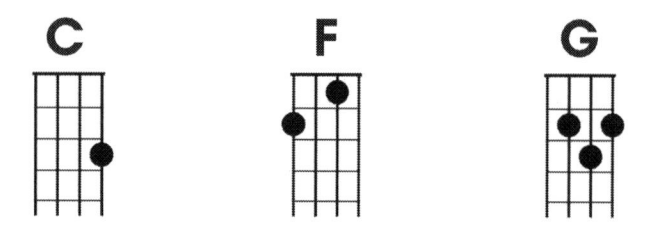

## Twinkle, Twinkle Little Star

Twin-kle, twin-kle, lit-tle star, how I won-der what you are.

Up a-bove the world so high, like a di-amond in the sky.

Twin-kle, twin-kle, lit-tle star, how I won-der what you are!

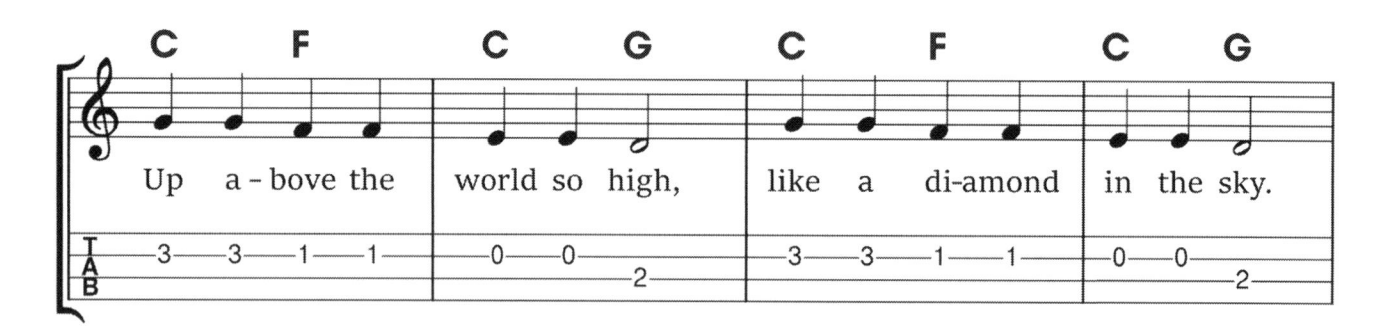

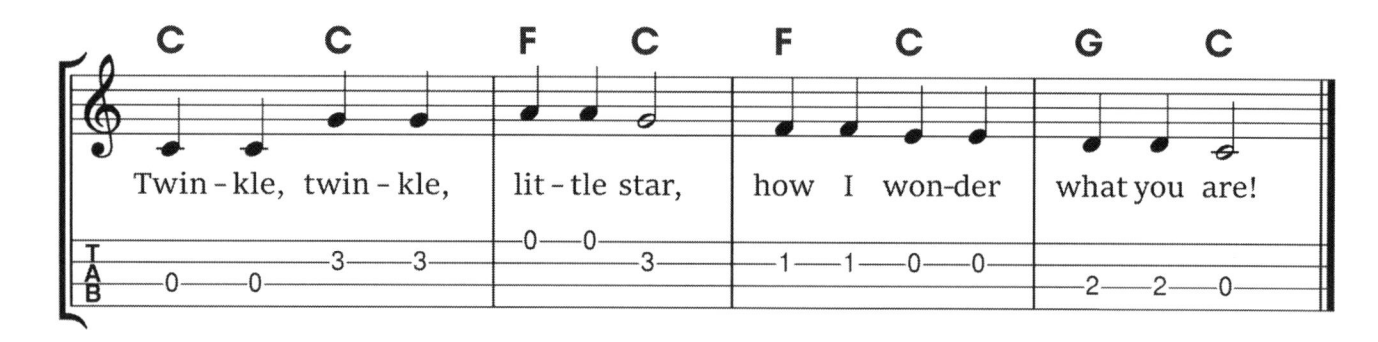

Don't forget to check out my YouTube Channel **Pierre Hache Music** for **FREE** play-along videos and practice tips to complement this book!

## Ode to Joy

*Once you get the hang of the tricky **E** chord on p. 37, come back and try it here. It sounds great!

## Mary Had a Little Lamb

Ma-ry had a little lamb, little lamb, little lamb.

Ma-ry had a little lamb whose fleece was white as snow.

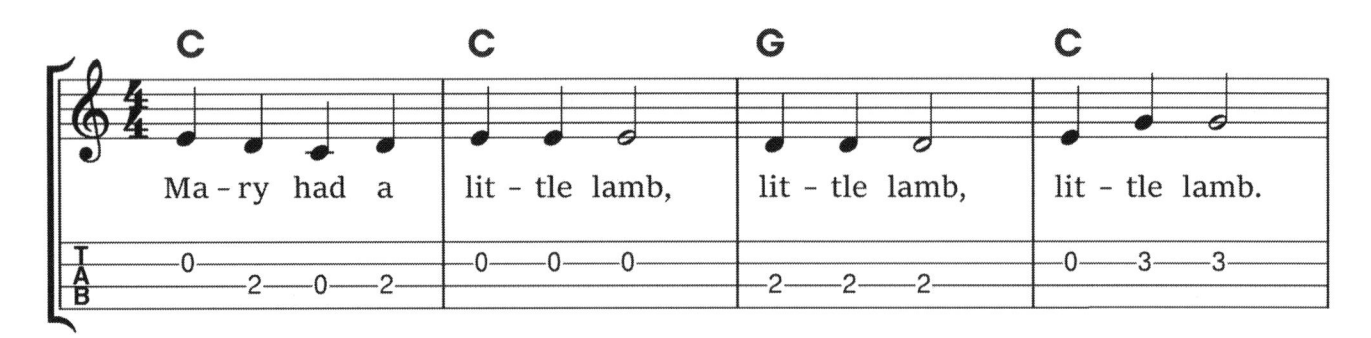

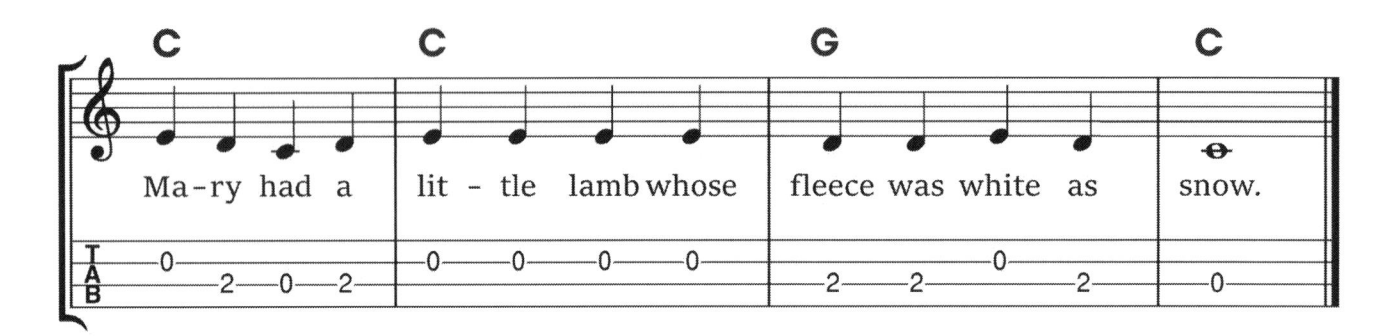

Notice the half note followed by a dot at the end of **London Bridge**. A dotted half note lasts 3 beats. You'll see more of these in the *Waltz Time* section (p. 31).

You can try this one with **2 strums** per chord, as indicated by the dotted arrows. The **(...)** means to continue the suggested strumming pattern.

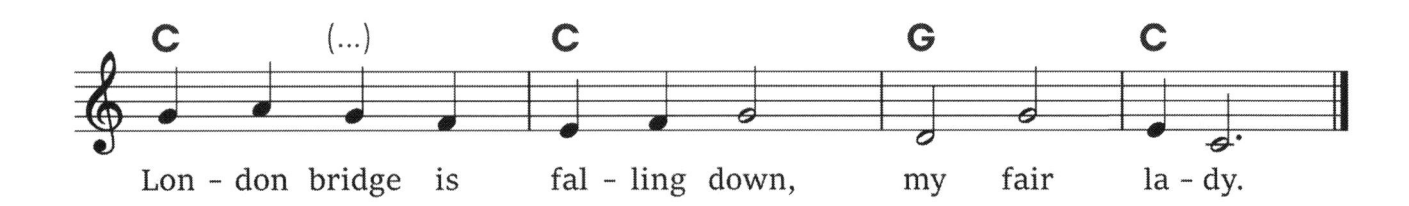

## London Bridge

Lon-don bridge is fal-ling down, fal-ling down, fal-ling down!

Lon-don bridge is fal-ling down, my fair la-dy.

27

# PICKUPS AND TIES

Sometimes melodies start *before* the first beat of a song. The notes leading up to beat **1** are called pickup notes.

Count the missing beats before playing the pickups in the following exercises.

A tie is a curved line connecting two notes. It means to let the first note ring through the second. Ties often result in long notes that overlap bar lines.

Try the following examples. Pluck and hold the first of the two tied notes. Count the duration of both notes *without* plucking the second.

The pickup in **When the Saints Go Marching In** starts on beat **2**.
Make sure to let the tied notes ring for their full duration.

Once you can play the melody, sing and strum along!

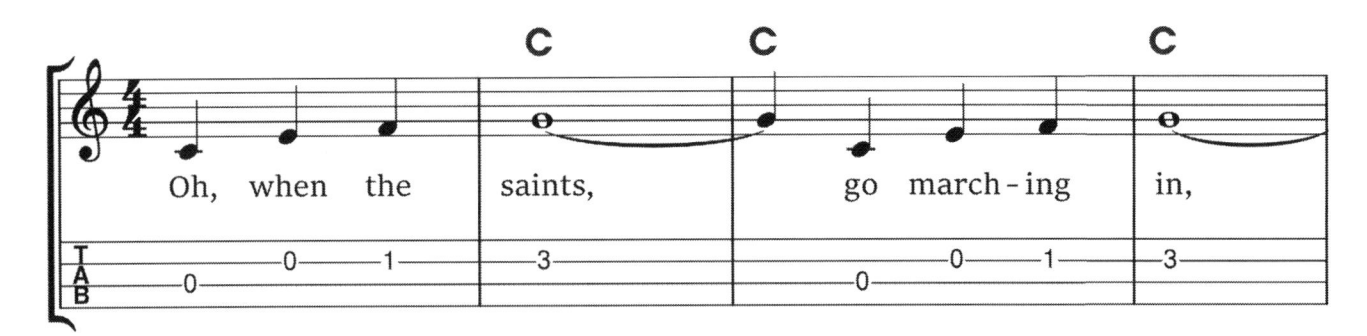

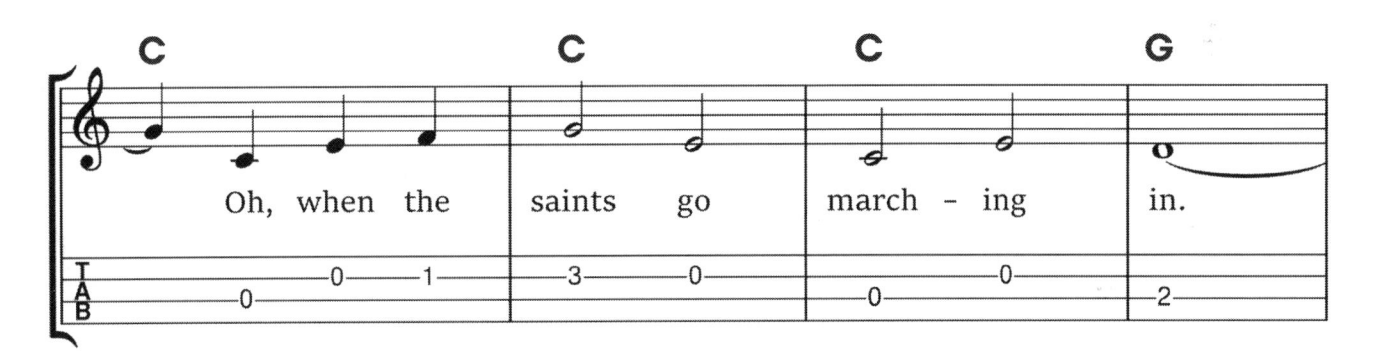

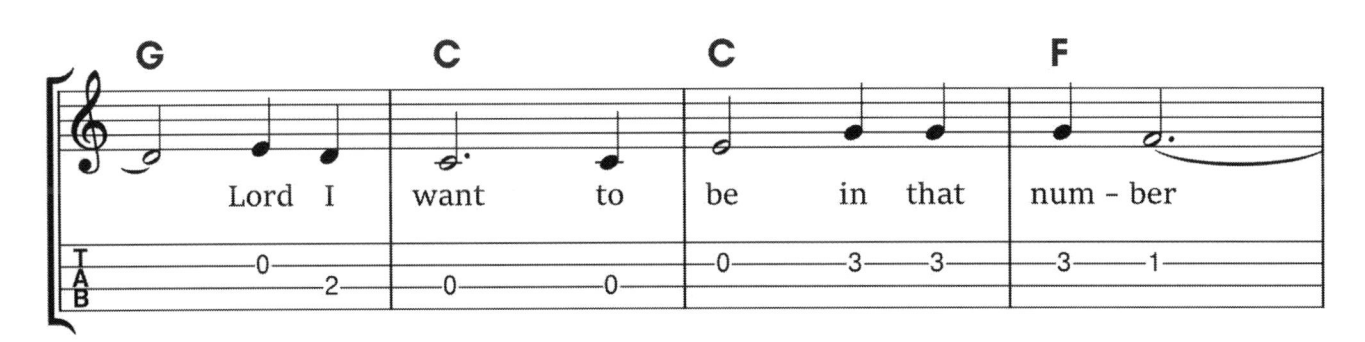

## When the Saints Go Marching In

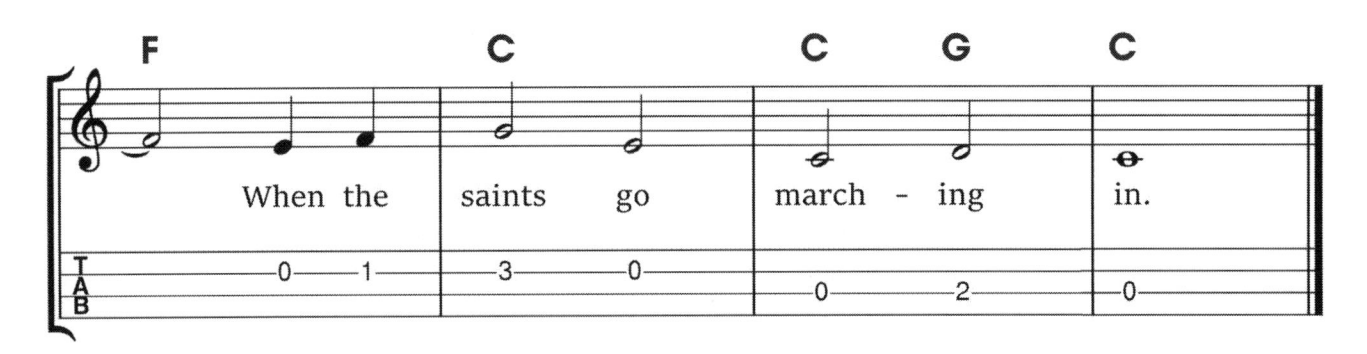

# WALTZ TIME

Waltz time, or 3/4, has 3 quarter notes per measure. This time signature has a distinct bouncy, rolling feel to it.

Say the following phrase slowly to help internalize the waltz feel:
*Oom-pah-pah Oom-pah-pah Oom-pah-pah Oom-pah-pah . . .*

Notice that **dotted half notes** (𝅗𝅥.), worth **3 beats**, last a full measure in 3/4.

Play the following rhythms on your **A** string while counting out loud.
You can also try them on other strings.

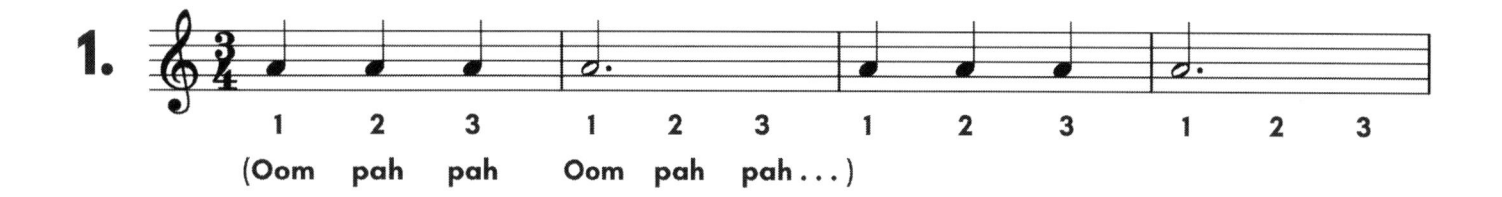

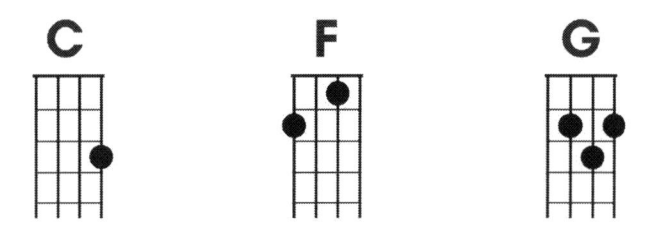

## Humpty Dumpty

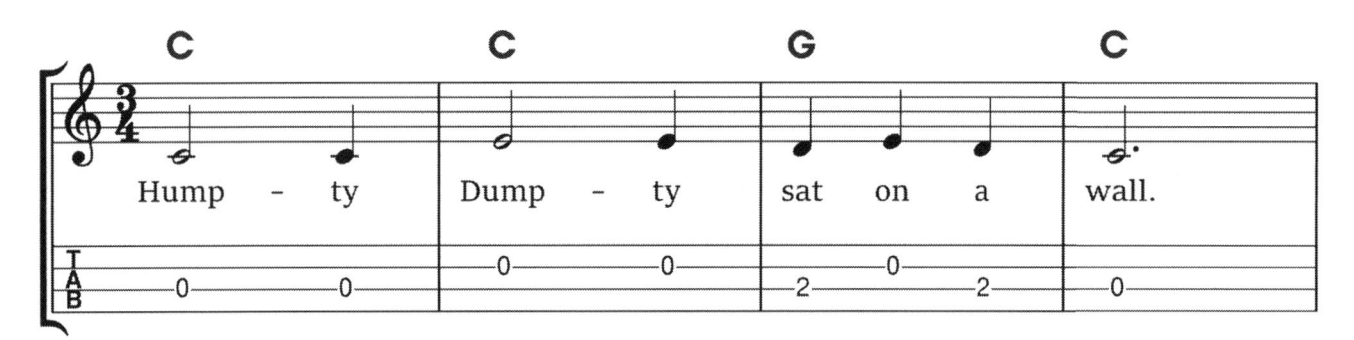

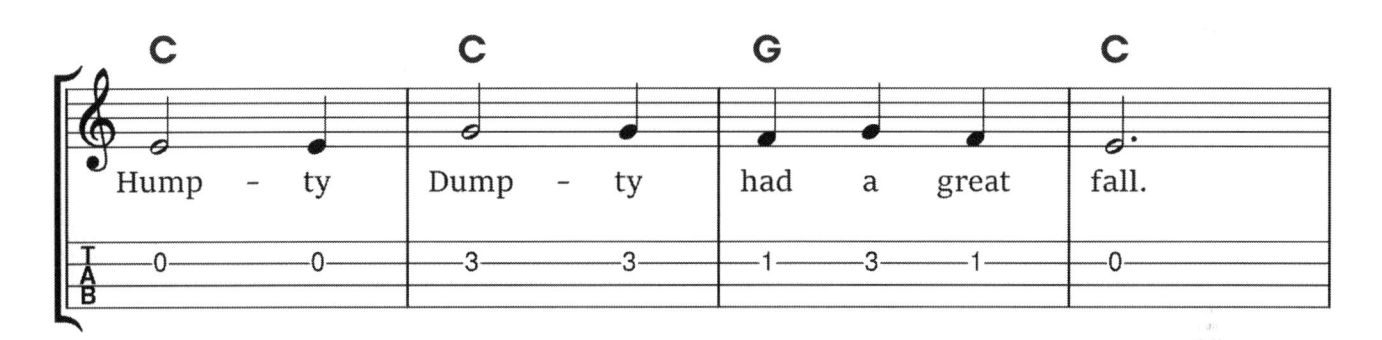

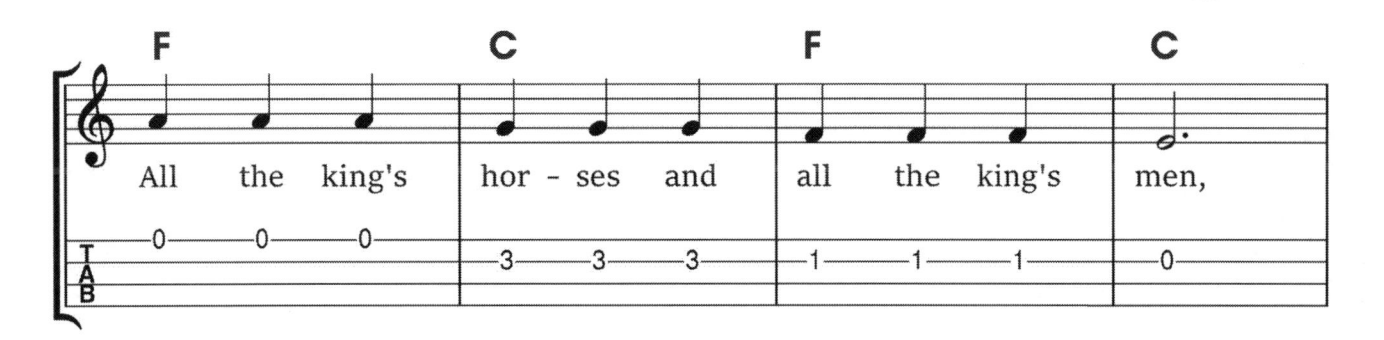

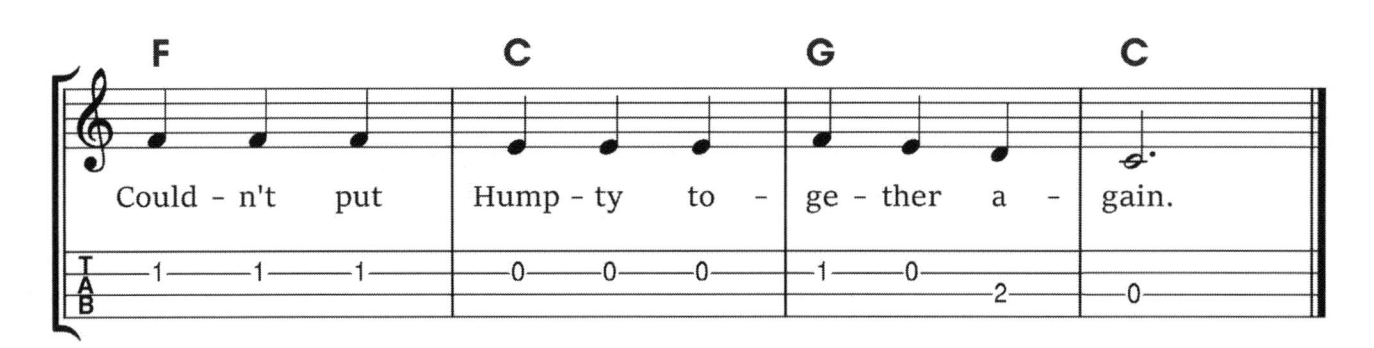

Hump-ty Dump-ty sat on a wall.
Hump-ty Dump-ty had a great fall.
All the king's hor-ses and all the king's men,
Could-n't put Hump-ty to-ge-ther a-gain.

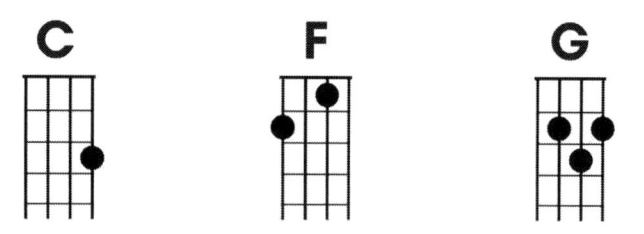

# For He's a Jolly Good Fellow

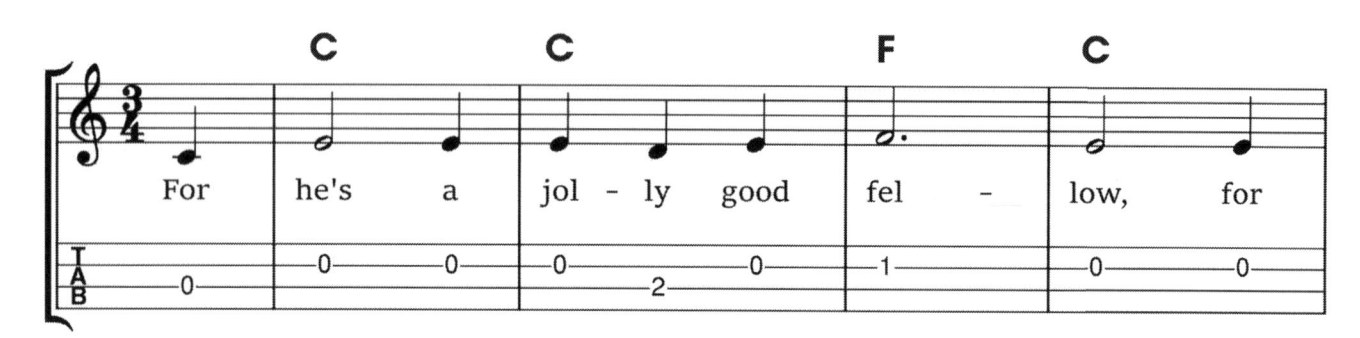

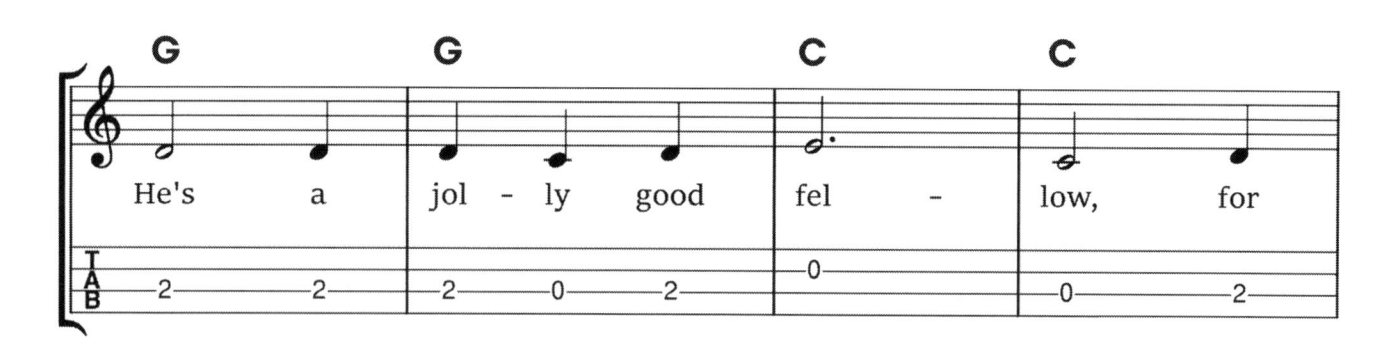

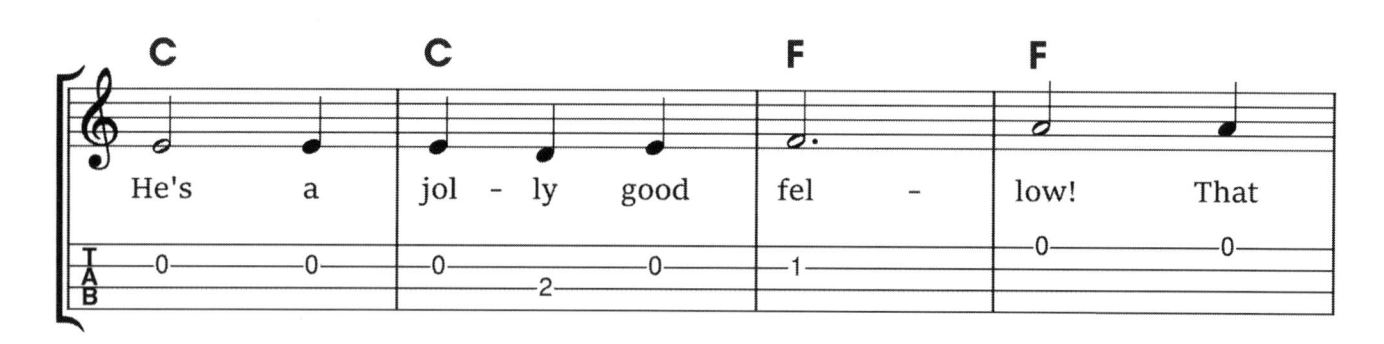

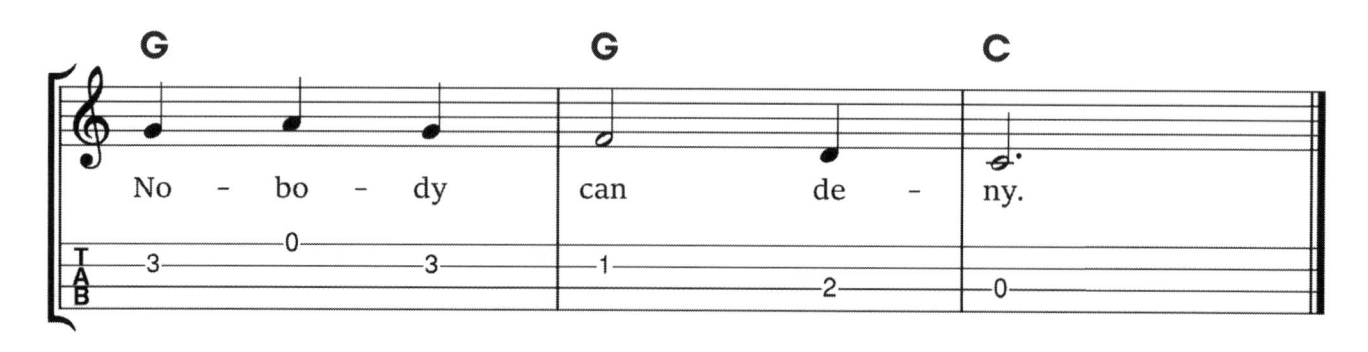

# EIGHTH NOTES

Eighth notes are joined by a horizontal bar and are faster than quarter notes. You can fit two eighth notes in the space of one quarter note. To play eighth notes, start by counting to 4 with an "and" between each beat.

*1 and 2 and 3 and 4 and 1 and 2 and 3 and 4 and ...*

Now, pluck your **A** string on every count, including the "and"s (shown as **&** in the exercises). There should be 8 even notes per measure.

1 & 2 & 3 & 4 & 1 & 2 & 3 & 4 &

The following exercises combine eighth notes and quarter notes. Play the "and"s for the eighth notes, but count the "and" without plucking for the quarter notes.

1. 1 & 2 & 3 & 4 & 1 & 2 & 3 & 4 & 1 & 2 & 3 & 4 & 1 & 2 & 3 & 4 &

2. 1 & 2 & 3 & 4 & 1 & 2 & 3 & 4 & 1 & 2 & 3 & 4 & 1 & 2 & 3 & 4 &

3. 1 & 2 & 3 & 4 &...

4.

34

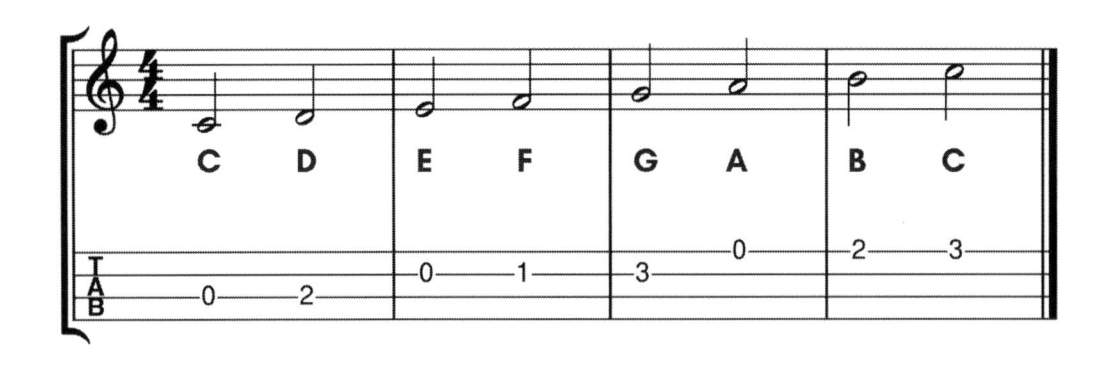

## This Old Man

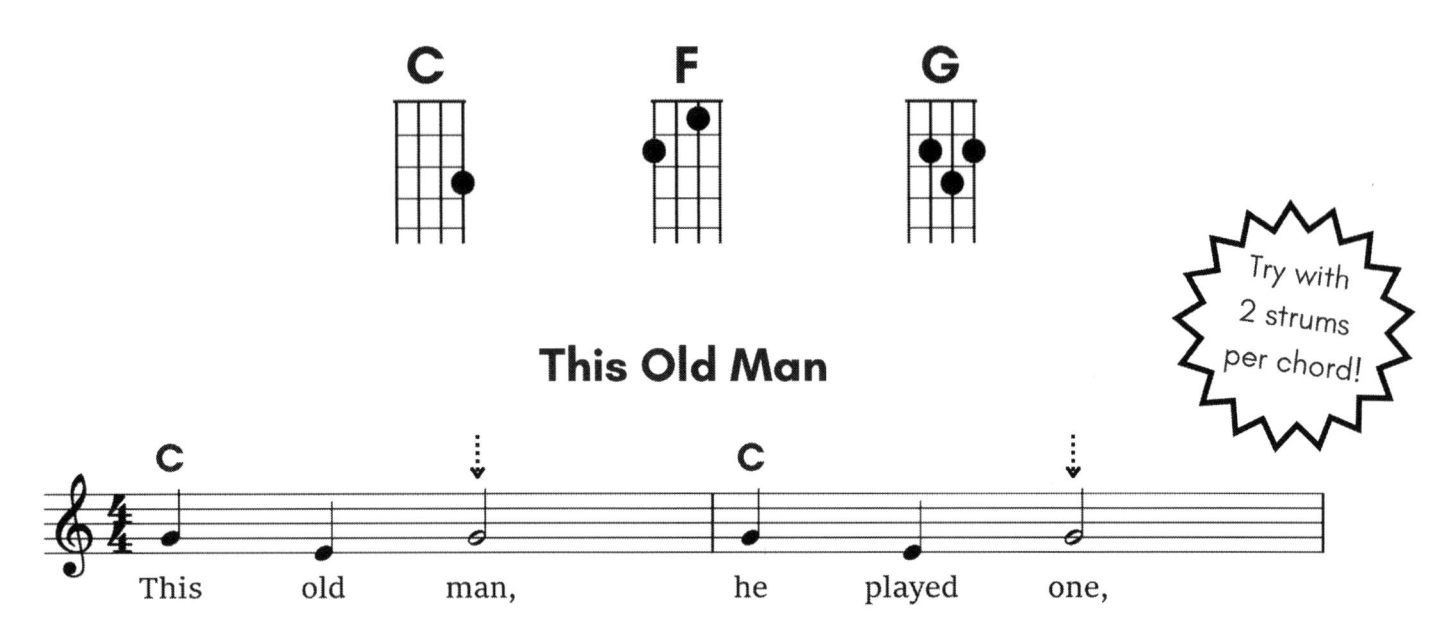

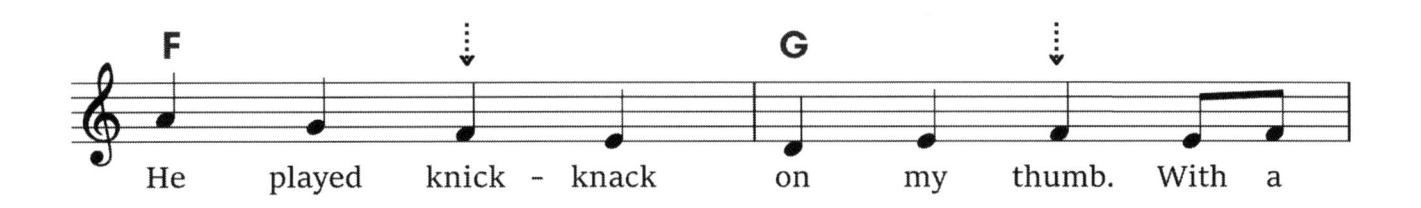

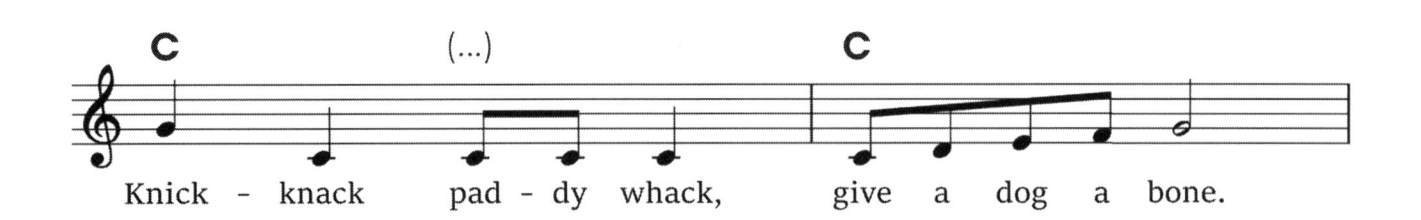

*Try with 2 strums per chord!*

**C** This old man, he played **C** one,
**F** He played knick-knack **G** on my thumb. With a
**C** Knick-knack paddy whack, **C** give a dog a bone.
**G** This old man came **G** rolling **C** home.

## Baa Baa Black Sheep

| C | C | F | C |

Baa, baa, black sheep, have you a-ny wool?

| F | C | G | C |

Yes sir, yes sir, three bags full.

| C | F | C | G |

One for the mas-ter, one for the dame,

| C | F | C | G |

One for the lit-tle boy who lives down the lane.

| C | C | F | C |

Baa, baa, black sheep, have you a-ny wool?

| F | C | G | C |

Yes sir, yes sir, three bags full.

---

I hope you're having fun so far! If you're getting value from this book, please consider leaving a positive review on **Amazon**. Every review really helps with sales and visibility. Help bring the JOY of music into more homes. Thank you!!!

# MORE CHORDS

**C7**

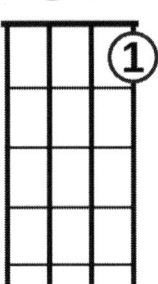

**A7**

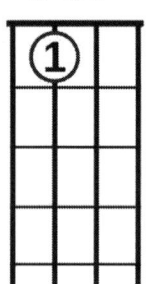

**D7**

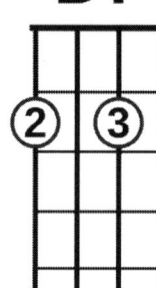

**G7**

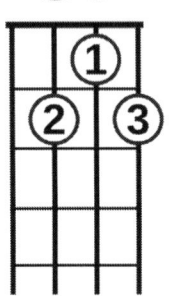

**Gm**

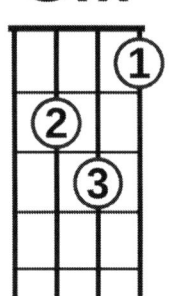

**Dm**

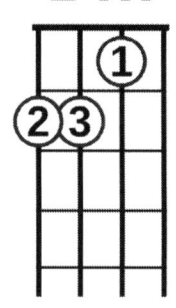

**Em**

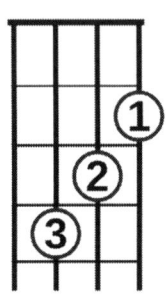

**A**

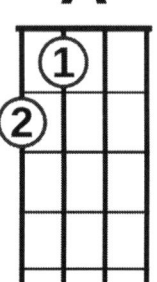

**D**

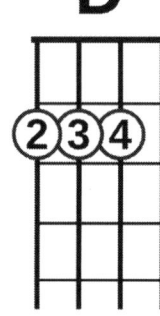

**E**

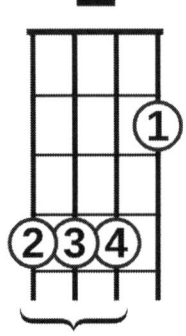

**B♭**

**B♭6**

Play top 3 strings for an easier version

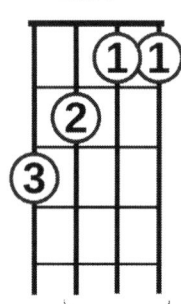

Play bottom 3 strings for an easier version

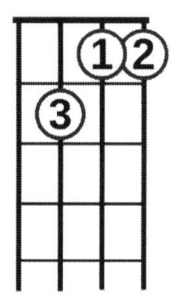

# STRUMMING PATTERNS

To develop a flow to your strumming, repeat the following exercise at least 20 times. Begin by counting full measures of eighth notes:

1 and 2 and 3 and 4 and 1 and 2 and 3 and 4 and . . .

With a relaxed wrist, gently strum down and up as you count over and over again. Every down should be on a number and every up on an "and".

↓ ↑ ↓ ↑ ↓ ↑ ↓ ↑
1 and 2 and 3 and 4 and . . .

The following are eight common strumming patterns. Slowly repeat each one many times on your favorite chords.

The "**m**" in patterns **3** and **4** means to *mute*, or gently slap the strings with your strumming hand. Count the "**&**"s outloud to help learn the rhythms correctly.

**1.**  ↓  ↓↑
    1  2 & 3  4

**2.**  ↓  ↓↑  ↑↓
    1  2 & 3 & 4

**3.**  m ↓ m ↓
    1 2 3 4

**4.**  m ↓ m ↑↓
    1 2 3 & 4

**5.**  ↓ ↓ ↓ ↓
    1 2 3 4

**6.**  ↓ ↓ ↓ ↓↑
    1 2 3 4 &

**7.**  ↓ ↓↑ ↑↓↑
    1 2 & 3 & 4 &

**8.**  ↓ ↓ ↑↓↑
    1 2 3 & 4 &

# CHORD PROGRESSIONS

Play the following chord progressions with the suggested strumming pattern. Once you can keep your rhythm steady and change chords on time, feel free to try different strumming patterns.

Refer to the **More Chords** section on p. 37 as needed. If certain chords give you trouble, try slowly switching between them 10 to 20 times with one strum.

1. F ↓ ↓↑ | C ↓ ↓↑ | G7 ↓ ↓↑ | C ↓ ↓↑
   1 2 3 4    1 2 3 4    1 2 3 4    1 2 3 4

2. G ↓ ↓↑ ↑↓ | D7 ↓ ↓↑ ↑↓ | G ↓ ↓↑ ↑↓ | C ↓ ↓↑ ↑↓
   1 2 3 4       1 2 3 4        1 2 3 4       1 2 3 4

Play the suggested strumming pattern once on each chord.

3. m ↓ m ↓     C  G  Am  F
   1 2 3 4

4. ↓ ↓ ↑↓↑     Am  Dm  G7  C
   1 2 3 4

5. ↓ ↓↑ ↑↓     Em  D  C  G
   1 2 3 4

39

The **E** and **B♭** (B flat) chords are challenging for all beginners. At first, try playing only the top three strings for the **E** chord, and the bottom three for **B♭**. You can also try replacing the **B♭** with a **B♭6**. (see p. 37)

It can be difficult to change chords quickly. Don't hesitate to slow down or play an easier strumming pattern. Be patient and work on the harder chords regularly.

**1.** ↓ ↓↑ ↑↓↑  G C G C
    1 2 3 4  G C D D

**2.** m ↓ m ↓  Am Em Am Em
    1 2 3 4  Am Em Dm G

**3.** m ↓ m ↑↓  A E A D
    1 2 3 4  A E D A

**4.** ↓ ↓↑ ↑↓  F B♭ F C
    1 2 3 4

**5.** ↓ ↓ ↓ ↓↑  Dm Dm B♭ F
    1 2 3 4

**6.** ↓ ↓ ↑↓↑  F A7 Dm B♭
    1 2 3 4

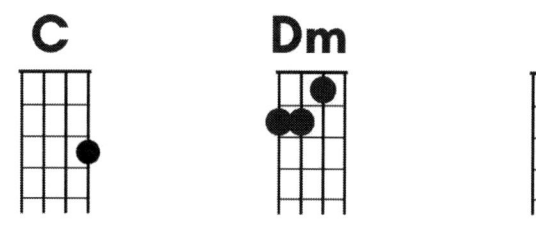

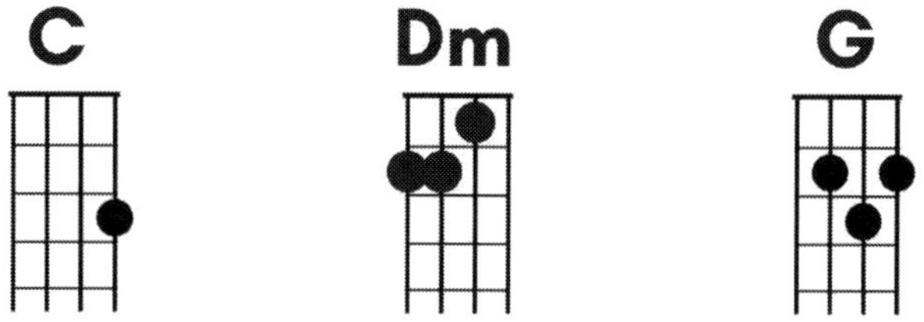

## It's Raining, It's Pouring

It's rain - ing, it's pour - ing, the old man is snor - ing. He
Bumped his head and went to bed and
Could - n't wake up in the morn - ing.

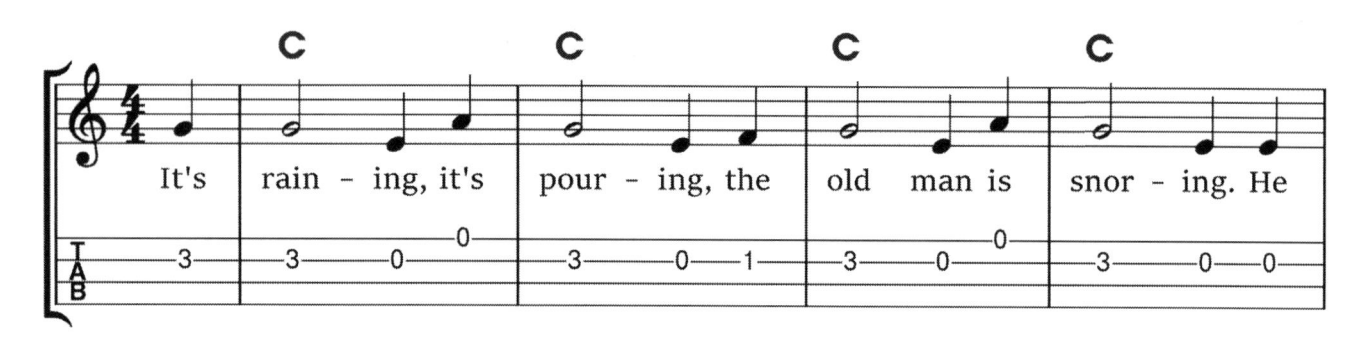

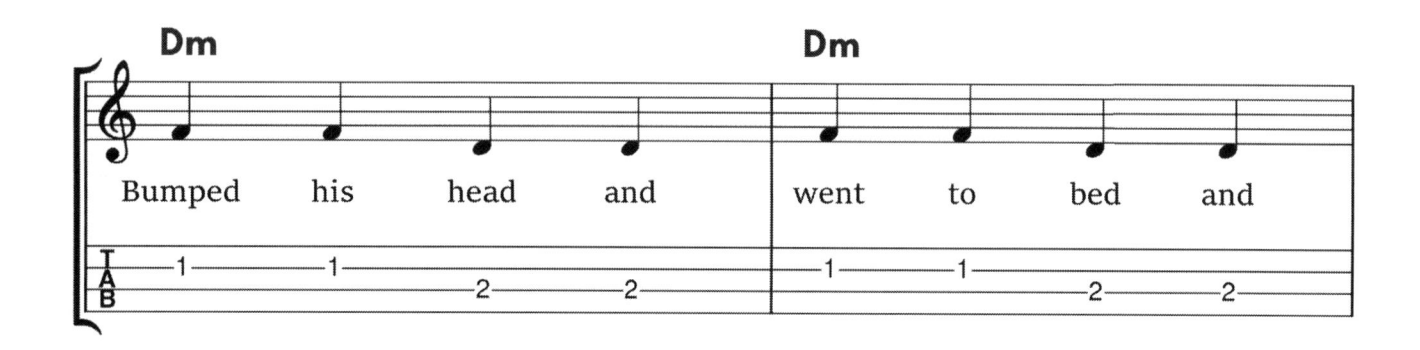

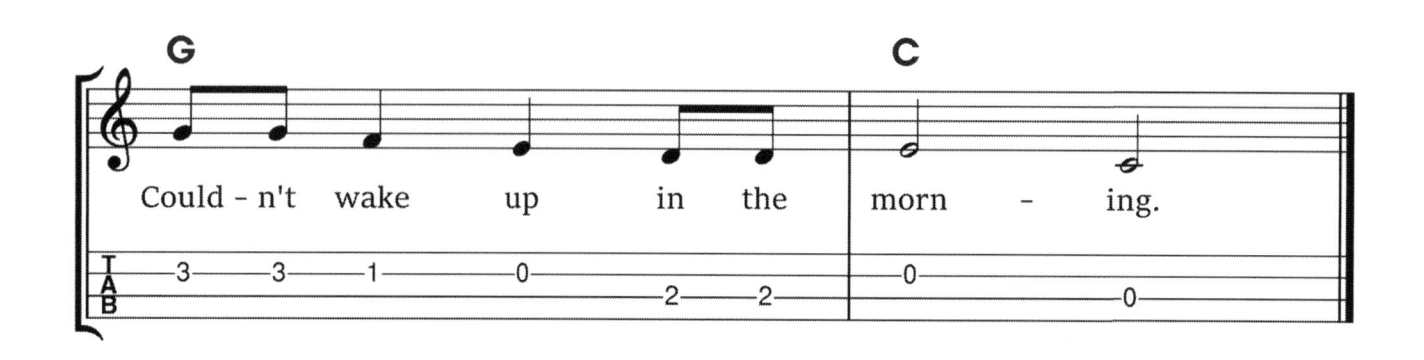

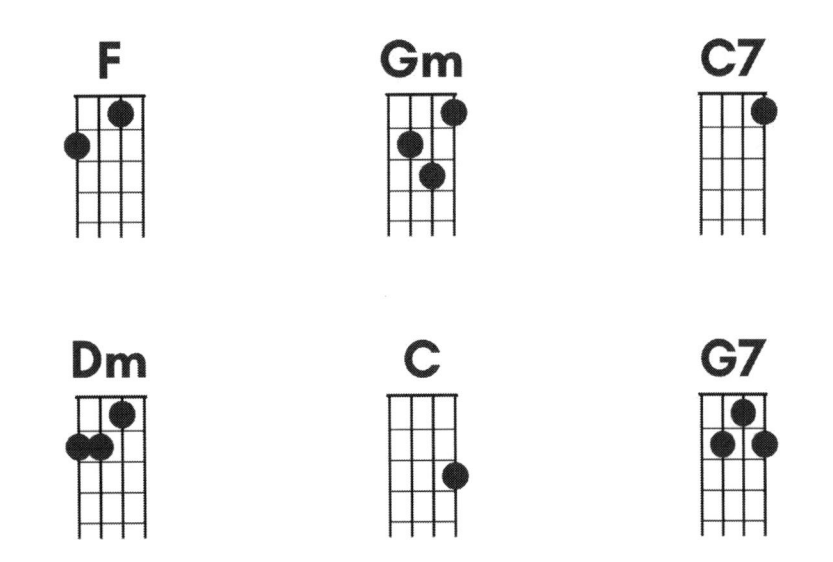

## Give My Regards to Broadway

| F | F | Gm | C7 |

Give my re - gards to Broad - way! Re -

| Gm | C7 | F | C7 |

mem - ber me to Her - ald Square! *Let ring 4 more beats*

| F | Dm | C | C |

Tell all the gang at For - ty Se - cond Street that

| G7 | C | F | |

I will soon be there!

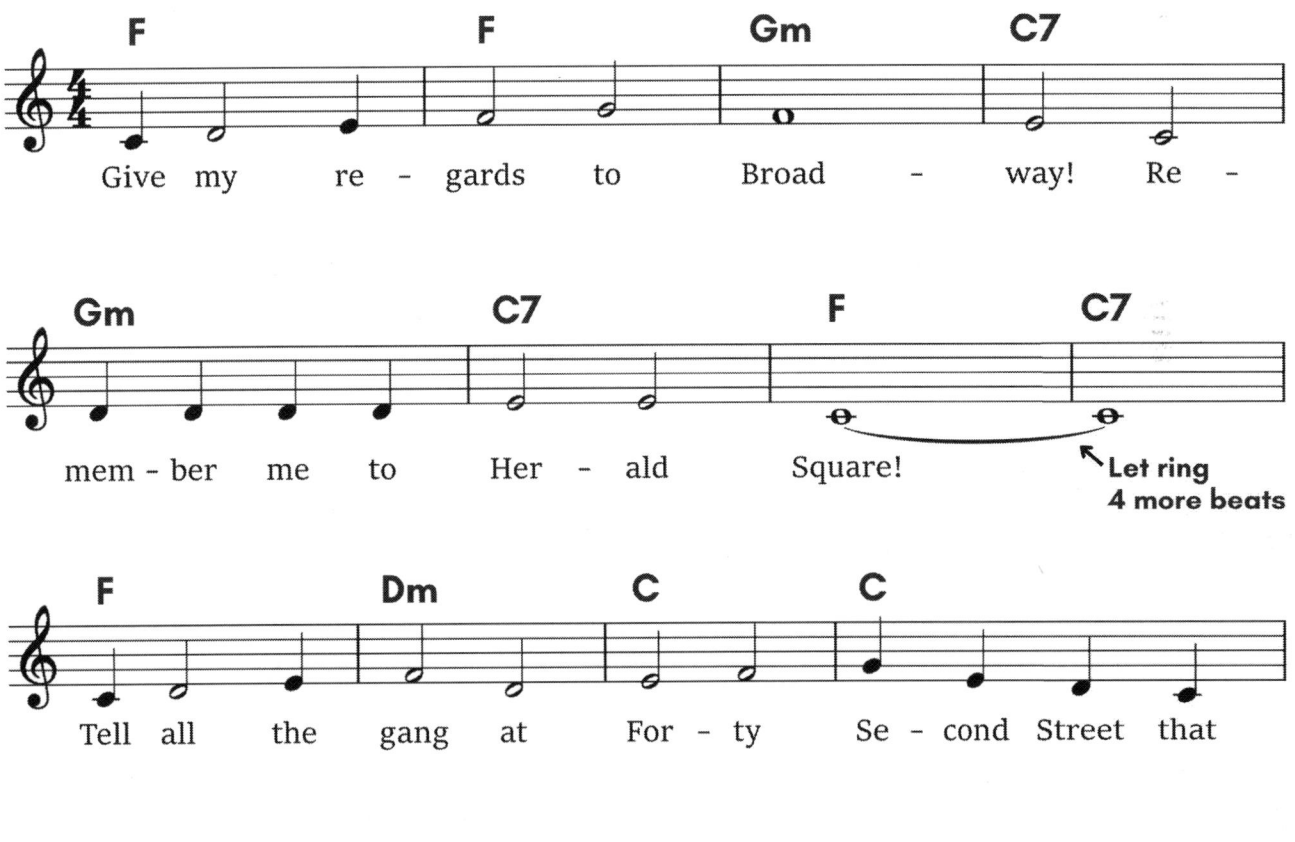

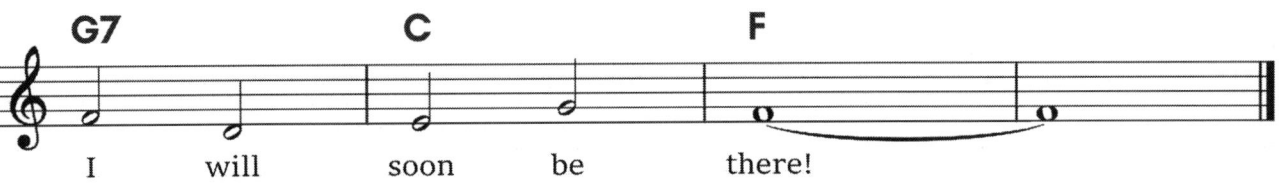

# B FLAT

The *key signature* of a song, located to the left of each staff, tells us to modify certain notes. A **sharp (#)** raises a note by one fret (towards the sound hole), whereas a **flat (♭)** lowers a note by one fret (towards the headstock).

The next group of songs are in the key of F, which has a **B flat**, indicated by the little "♭" to the left of the time signature. Notice the symbol is placed on the line of the **B** note. This means all the "**B**"s in the song have to be flattened, or played in the **1st** fret instead of the **2nd**.

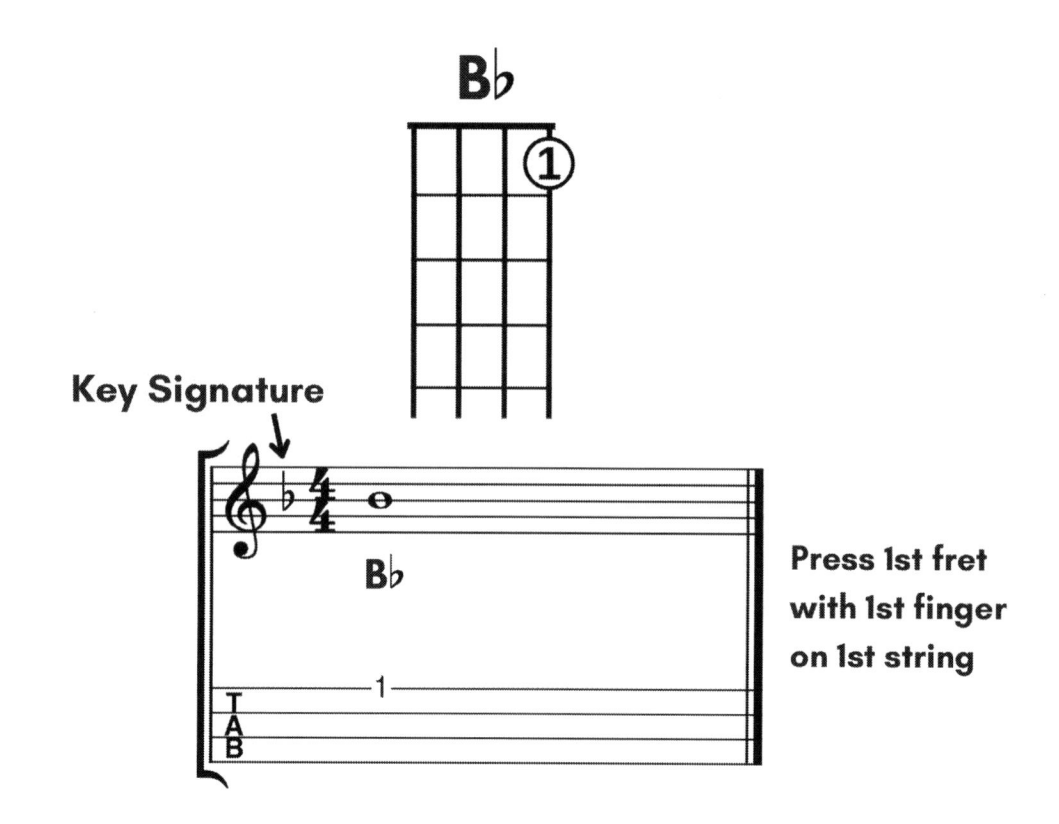

**Press 1st fret with 1st finger on 1st string**

Name the notes and play the following exercise.

At first, it can be tricky to remember to flatten every **B**. The flats are included before every **B** note in the next few songs as a reminder. However, note that sharps and flats are often only indicated at the beginning of each line.

Some of the following songs include the **B♭** chord. Remember, this challenging chord can be replaced with a **B♭6**, which some may find easier.

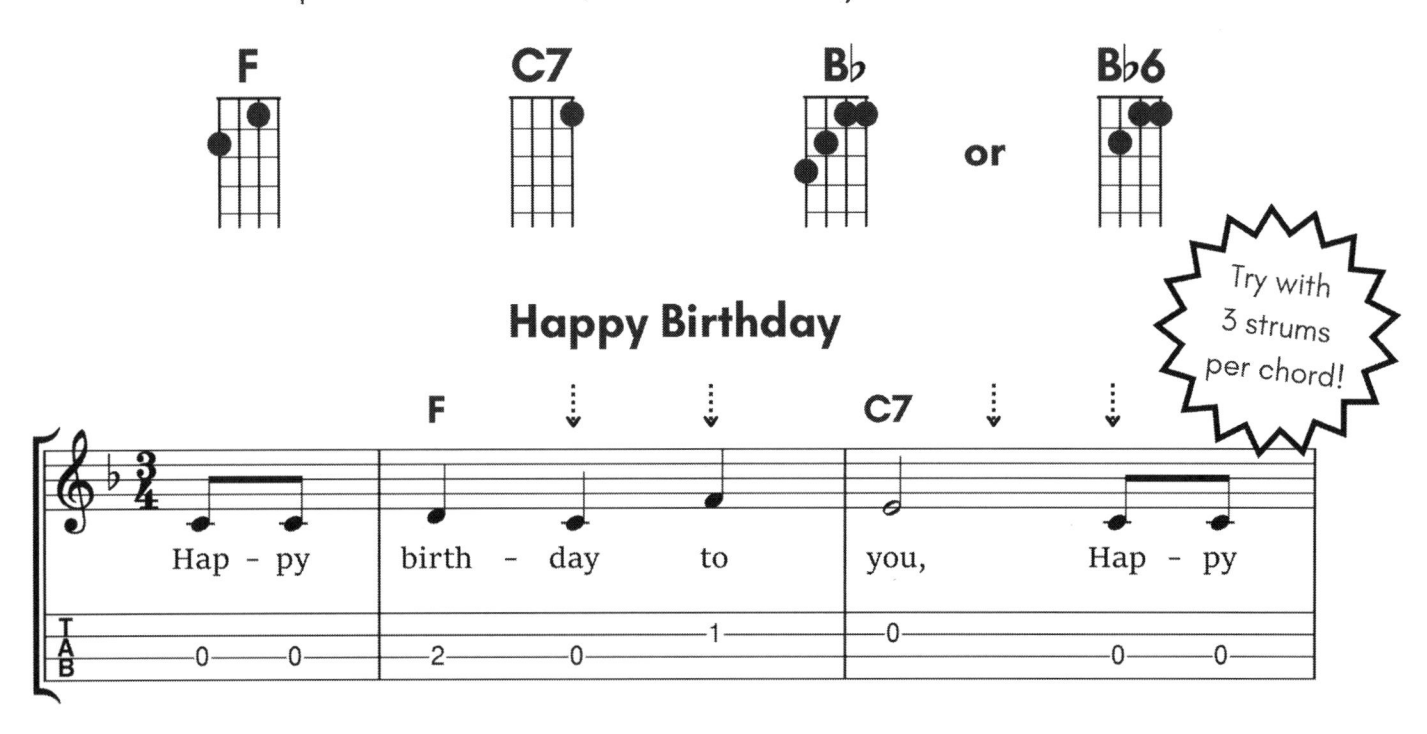

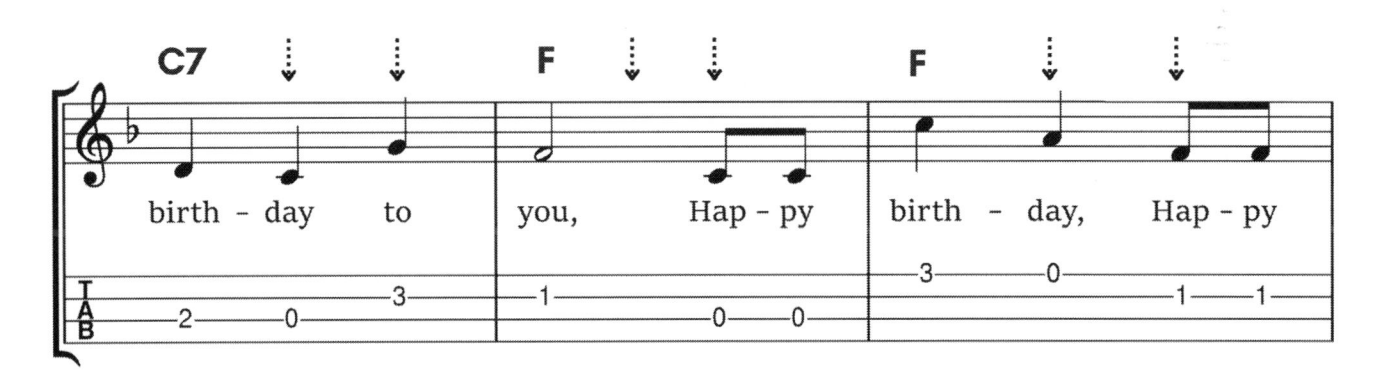

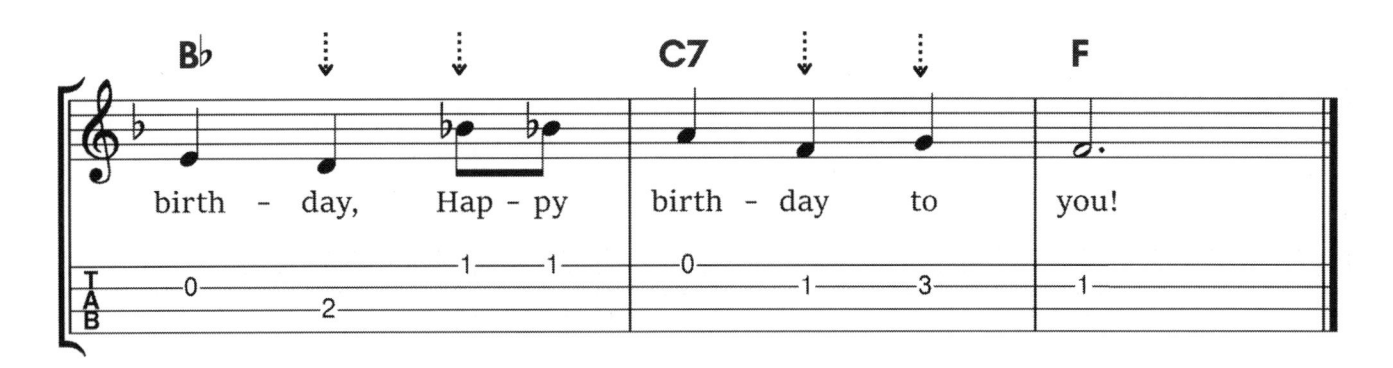

F          C7          B♭    or    B♭6

## Happy Birthday

*Try with 3 strums per chord!*

# Skip to My Lou

Skip, skip, skip to my Lou, skip, skip, skip to my Lou,

Skip, skip, skip to my Lou, skip to my Lou, my dar - ling.

# Yankee Doodle

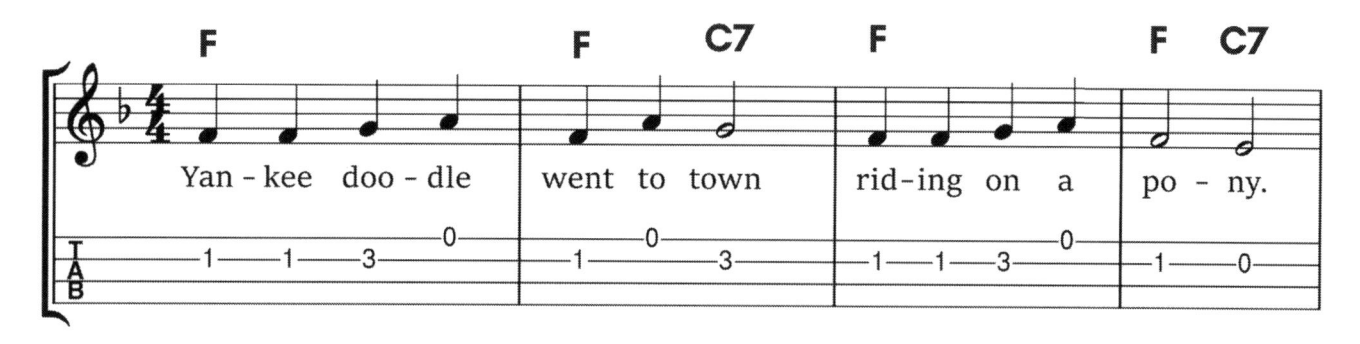

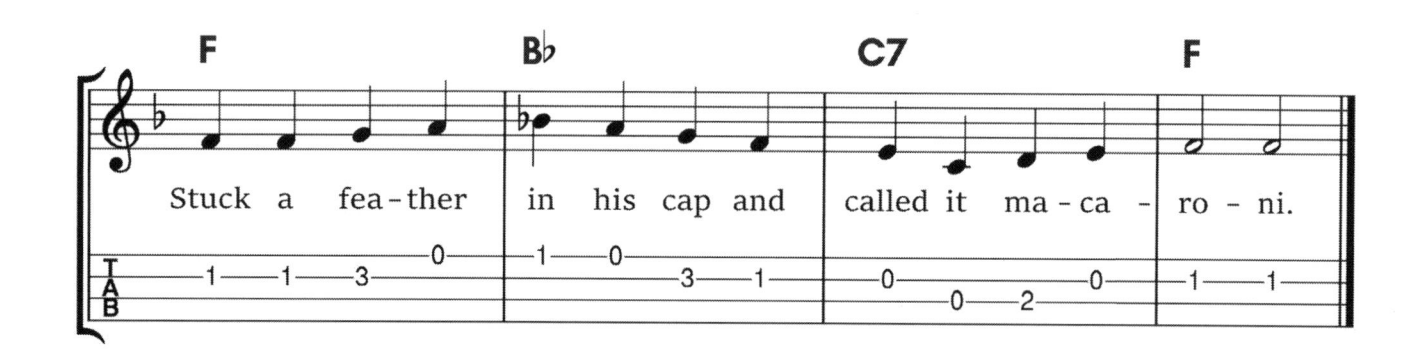

Yan - kee doo - dle went to town rid - ing on a po - ny.

Stuck a fea - ther in his cap and called it ma - ca - ro - ni.

Play the following songs without the TAB. Refer to the note summary as needed.

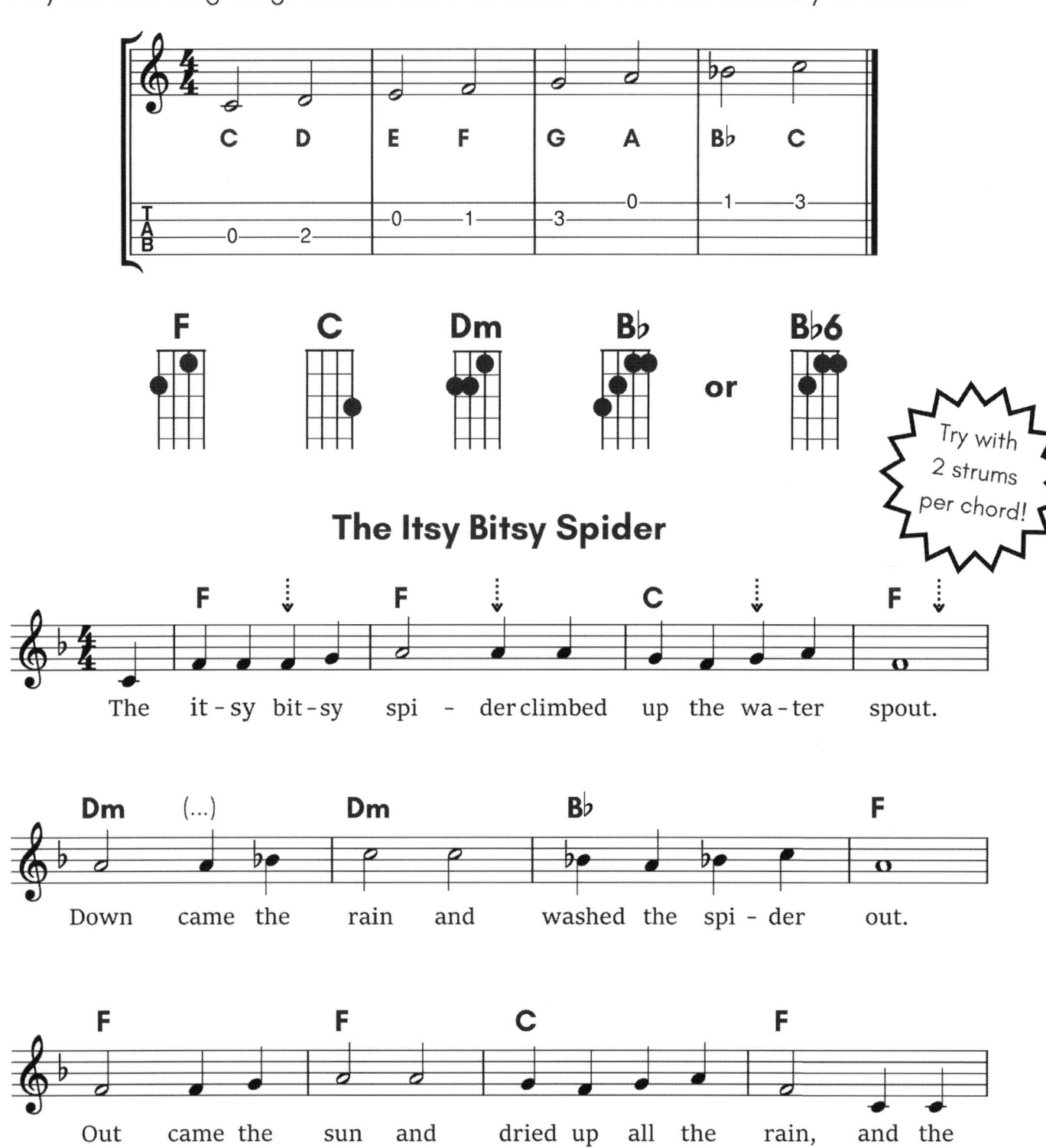

Notes: C D E F G A B♭ C

Chords: F, C, Dm, B♭, or B♭6

*Try with 2 strums per chord!*

## The Itsy Bitsy Spider

| F | F | C | F |

The it-sy bit-sy spi - der climbed up the wa-ter spout.

| Dm | (...) | Dm | B♭ | F |

Down came the rain and washed the spi-der out.

| F | F | C | F |

Out came the sun and dried up all the rain, and the

| F | F | C | F |

It-sy bit-sy spi - der climbed up the spout a - gain!

In the following songs, the **B flat** is only indicated in the **key signature**. Remember to flatten all the "**B**"s by playing them in the first fret.

## Bingo

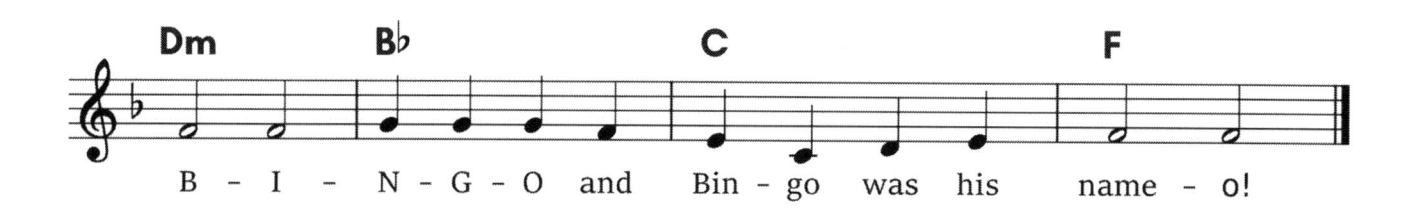

There was a farm-er had a dog and Bin-go was his name-o.
B - I - N - G - O, B - I - N - G - O,
B - I - N - G - O and Bin-go was his name - o!

## Down in the Valley

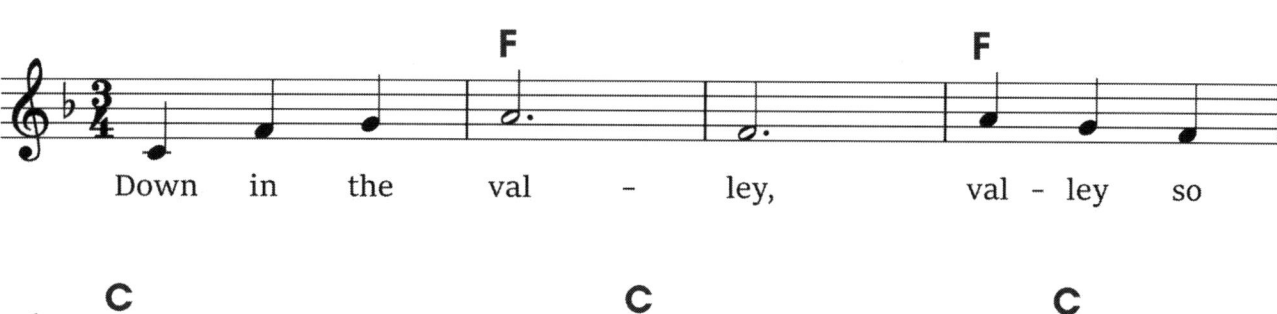

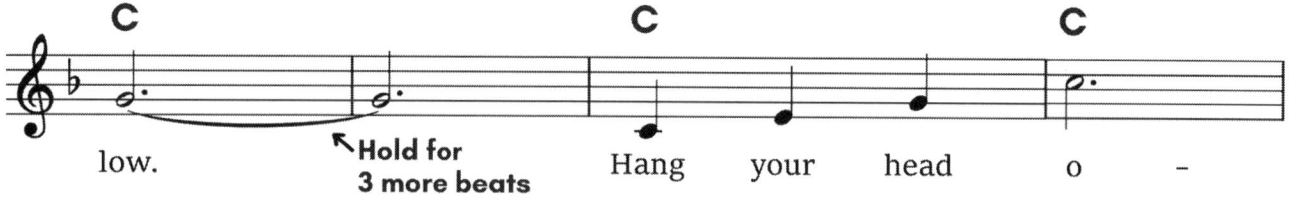

Down in the val - ley, val - ley so low. *Hold for 3 more beats* Hang your head o - ver, hear the wind blow.

47

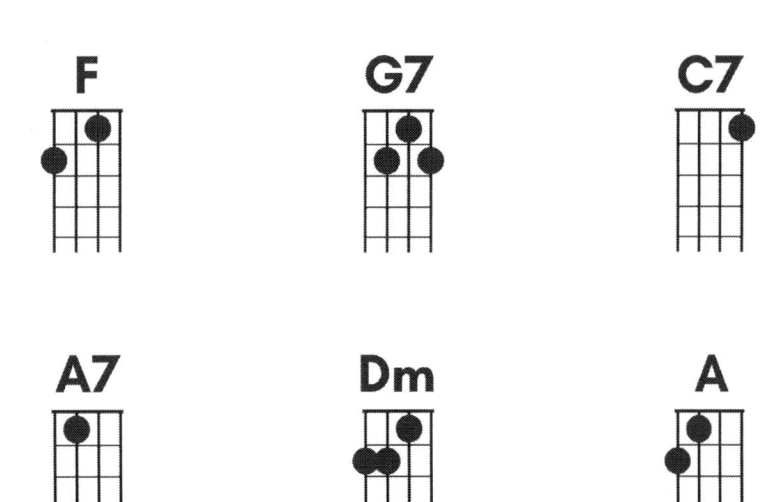

Once you can play this beautiful melody, hum and strum. ;)

*Try with 2 strums per chord!*

## Aura Lee

F    C    B♭    B♭6
          or

Dm    A7    A    Gm

## If You're Happy and You Know It

*Try with 2 strums per chord!*

**F** | **C**
If you're hap-py and you know it clap your hands! If you're

**C** | **F**
hap-py and you know it clap your hands! If you're

**B♭** (...) | **F**
hap-py and you know it and you real-ly want to show it, if you're

**C** | **F**
hap-py and you know it clap your hands!

49

# Hush Little Baby

Hush lit-tle ba-by don't say a word,

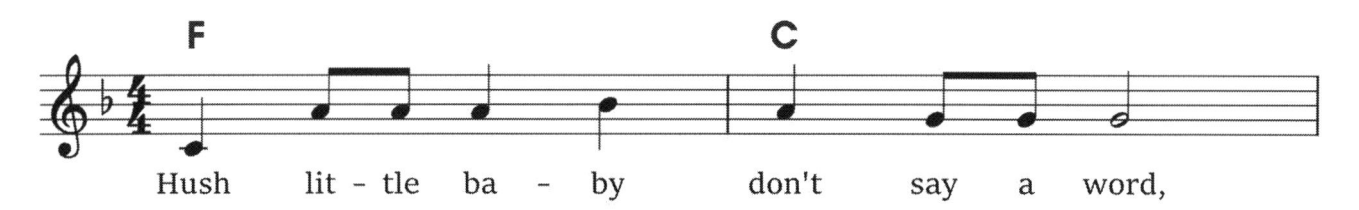

Ma-ma's gon-na buy you a mock-ing bird.

If that mock-ing bird don't sing,

Ma-ma's gon-na buy you a dia-mond ring.

# Snake Charmer

50

F  C7  G7  B♭  or  B♭6

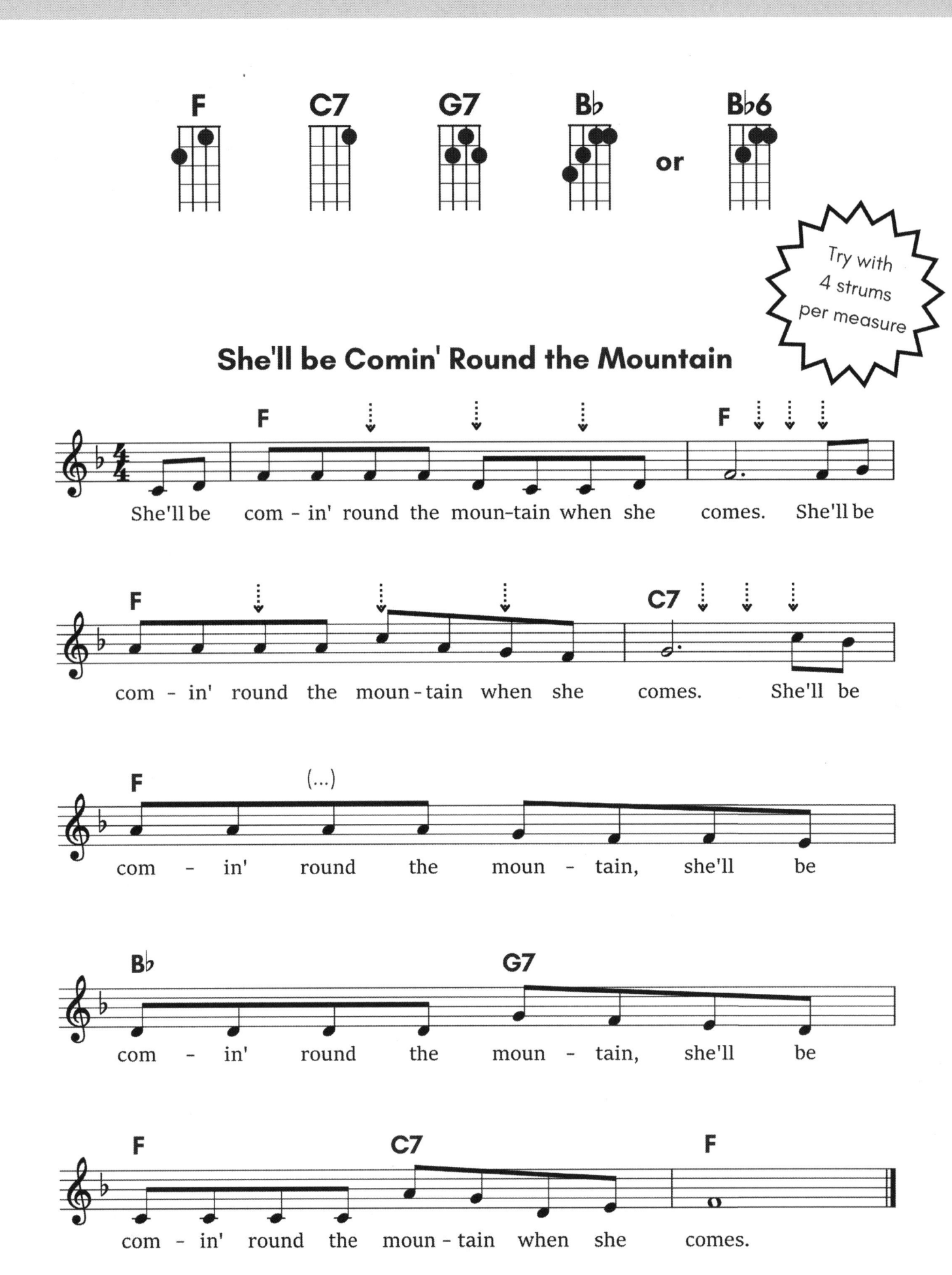

*Try with 4 strums per measure*

## She'll be Comin' Round the Mountain

F — She'll be com-in' round the moun-tain when she F — comes. She'll be

F — com-in' round the moun-tain when she C7 — comes. She'll be

F — com-in' round the moun-tain, she'll be

B♭ — com-in' round the moun-tain, G7 — she'll be

F — com-in' round the C7 — moun-tain when she F — comes.

51

# Rockin' Robin

*Try with ↓ ↓↑ ↑↓ on each chord!*

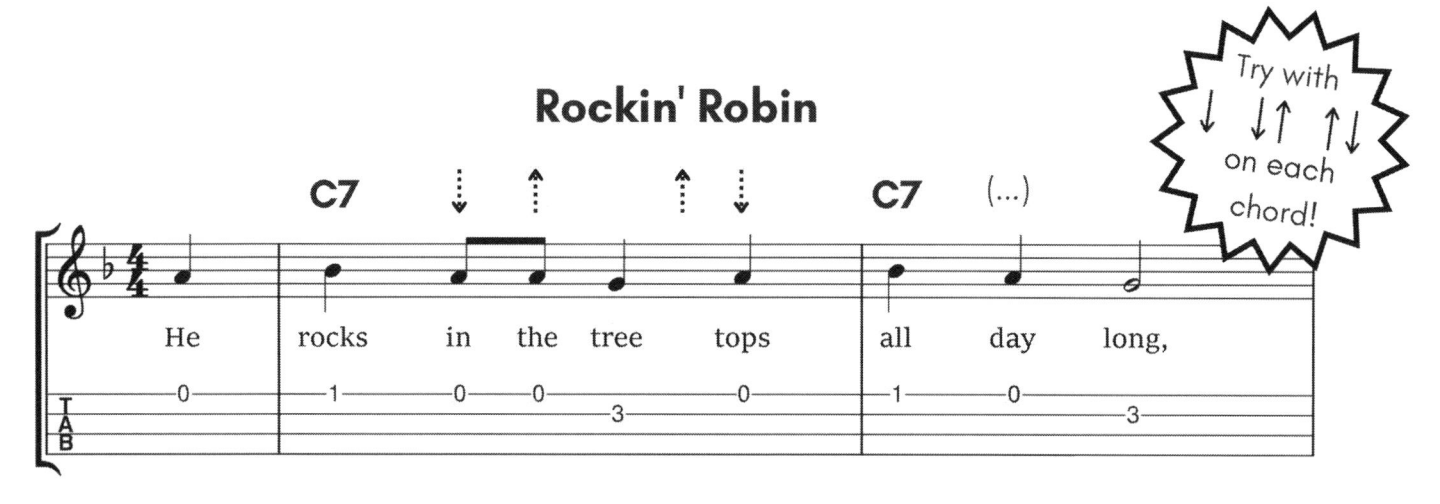

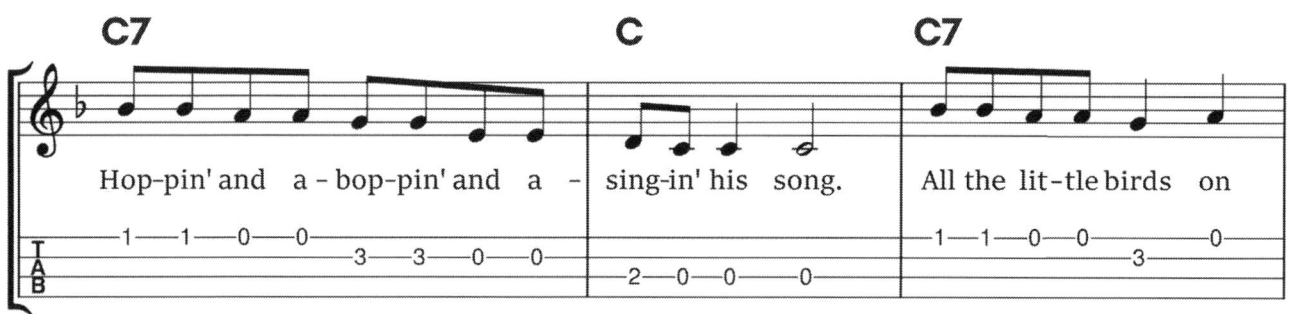

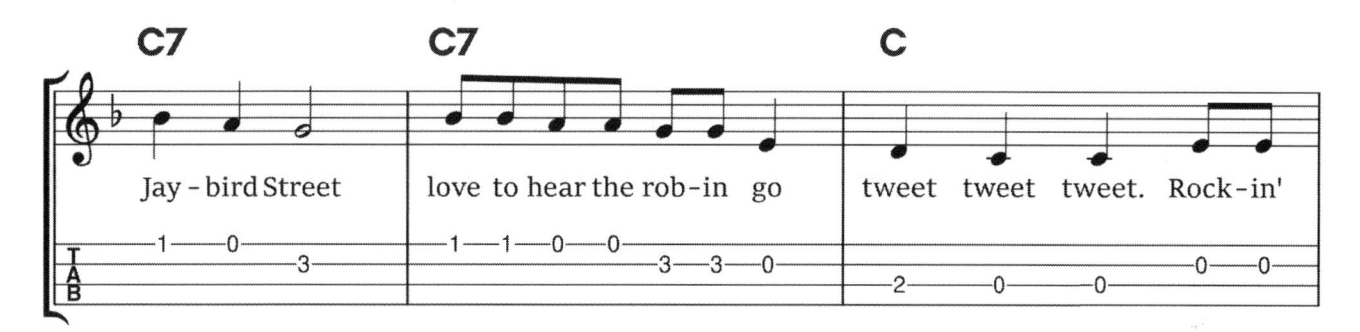

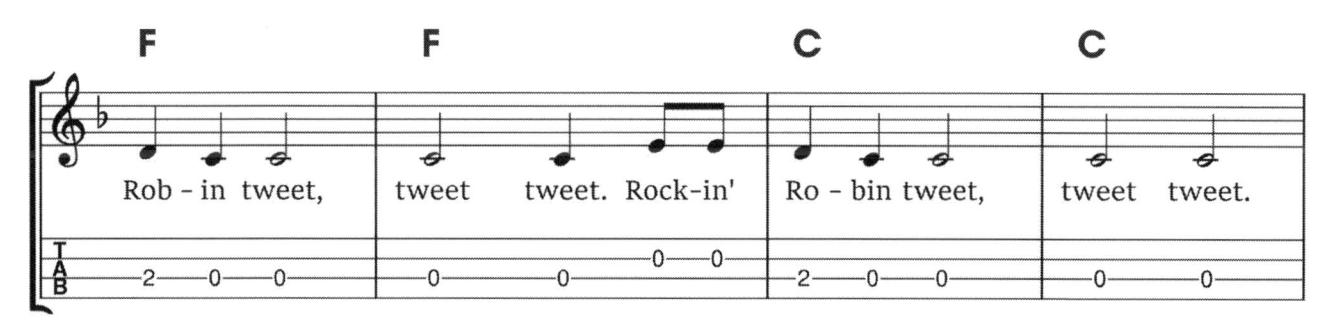

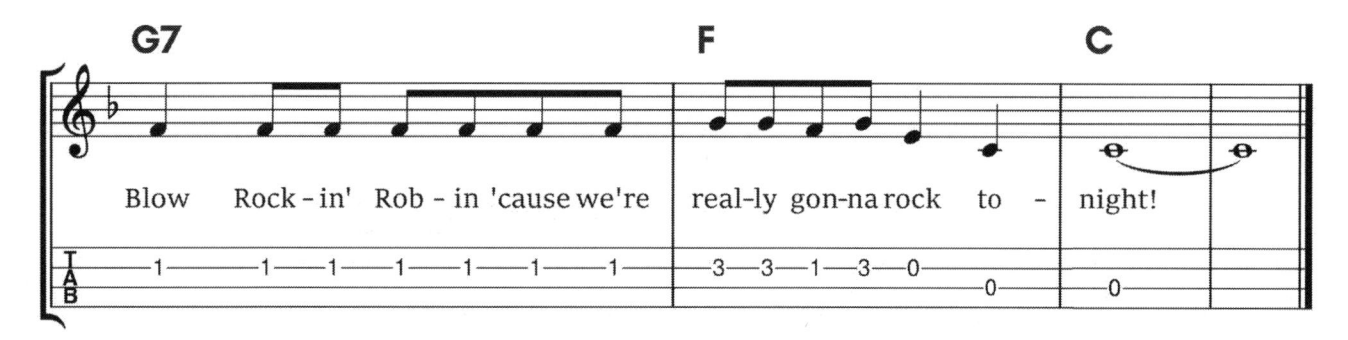

He rocks in the tree tops all day long,
Hop-pin' and a-bop-pin' and a-sing-in' his song.
All the lit-tle birds on Jay-bird Street
love to hear the rob-in go tweet tweet tweet.
Rock-in' Rob-in tweet, tweet tweet.
Rock-in' Ro-bin tweet, tweet tweet.
Blow Rock-in' Rob-in 'cause we're real-ly gon-na rock to-night!

# HIGH D

To play a **high D**, press the **5th** fret of the **1st** string with your pinky finger. There is often a fret marker, or a little dot, to indicate the **5th** fret on your ukulele.

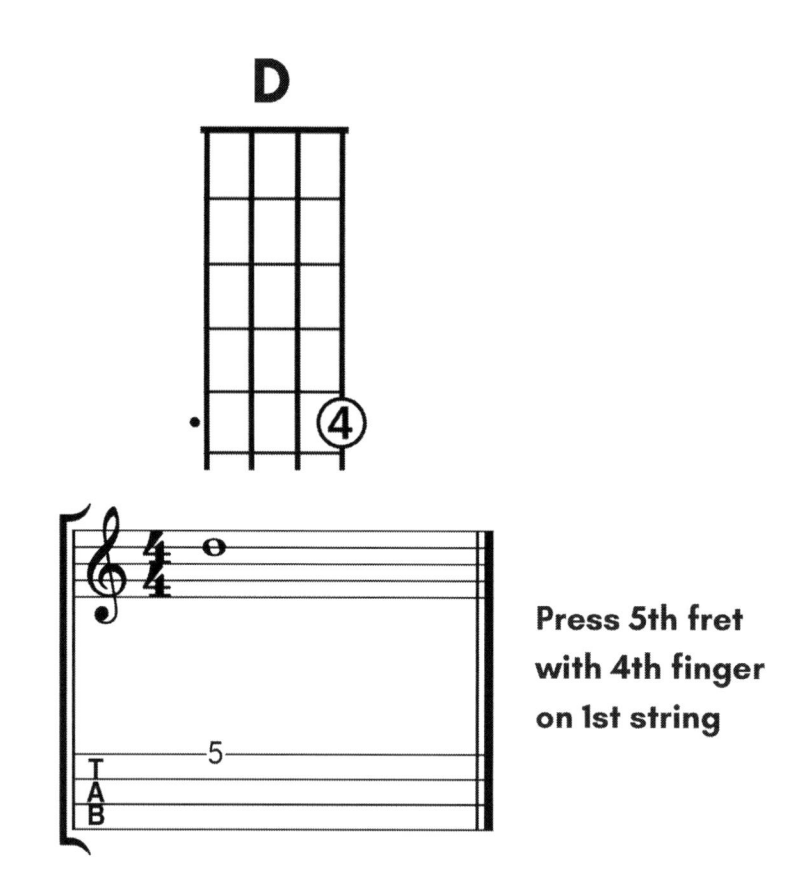

**Press 5th fret with 4th finger on 1st string**

Name the notes and play the following song. Notice the **high D** in the second line.

## Sea Shanty

**Amazing Grace**

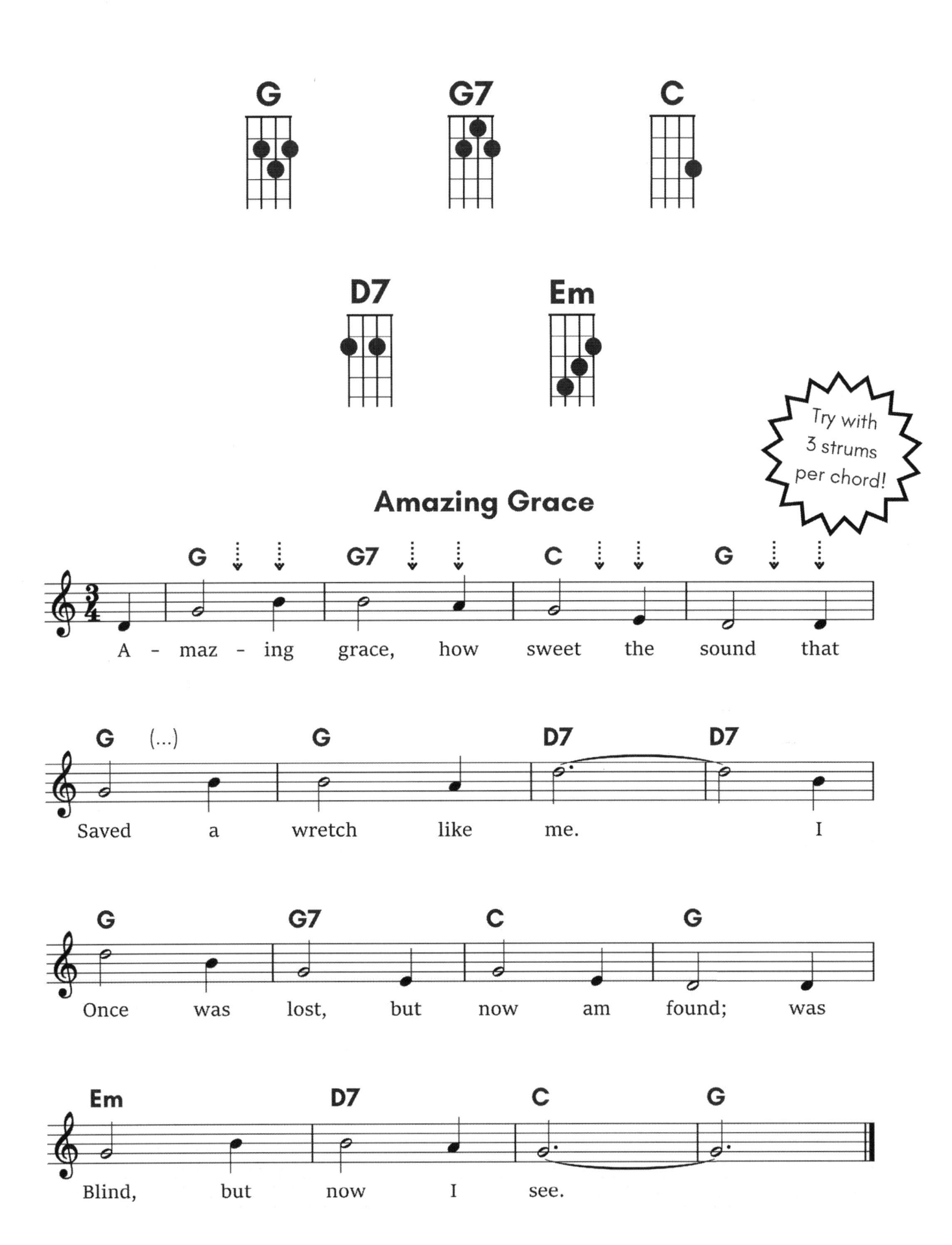

*Try with 3 strums per chord!*

| G | G7 | C | G |
|---|---|---|---|
| A - maz - ing | grace, how | sweet the | sound that |

| G (...) | G | D7 | D7 |
|---|---|---|---|
| Saved a | wretch like | me. | I |

| G | G7 | C | G |
|---|---|---|---|
| Once was lost, | but now | am found; | was |

| Em | D7 | C | G |
|---|---|---|---|
| Blind, but | now I | see. | |

54

This next song not only has a **high D**, but also a **G#** (2nd string, 4th fret) and an **F#** (2nd string, 2nd fret). Use the TAB to guide you and have fun!

## Take Me Out to the Ballgame

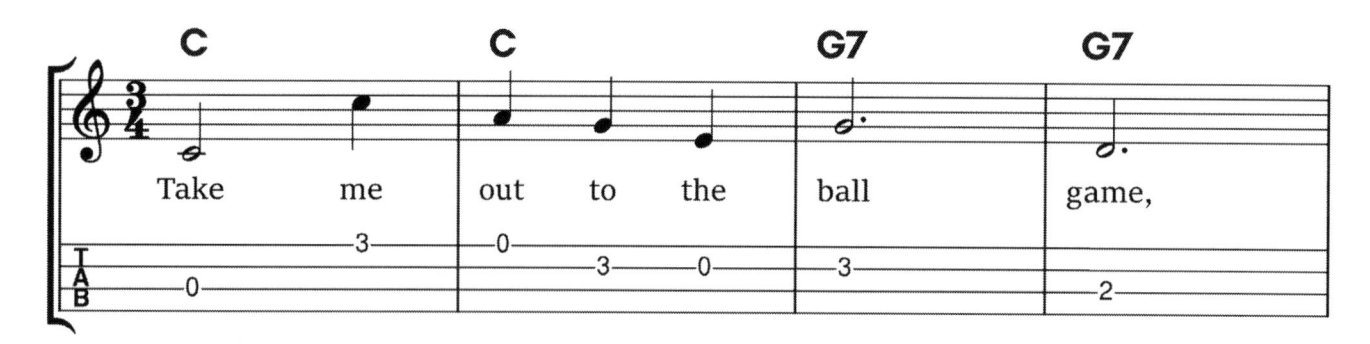

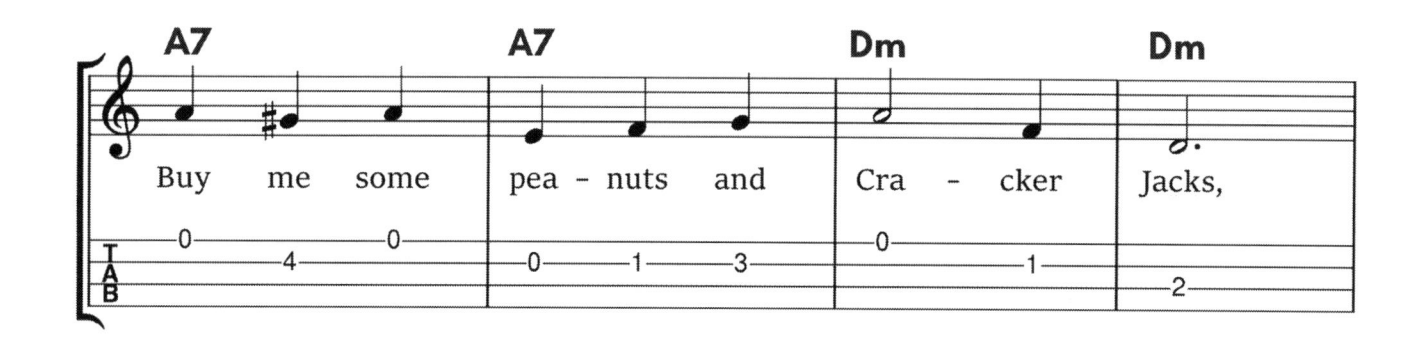

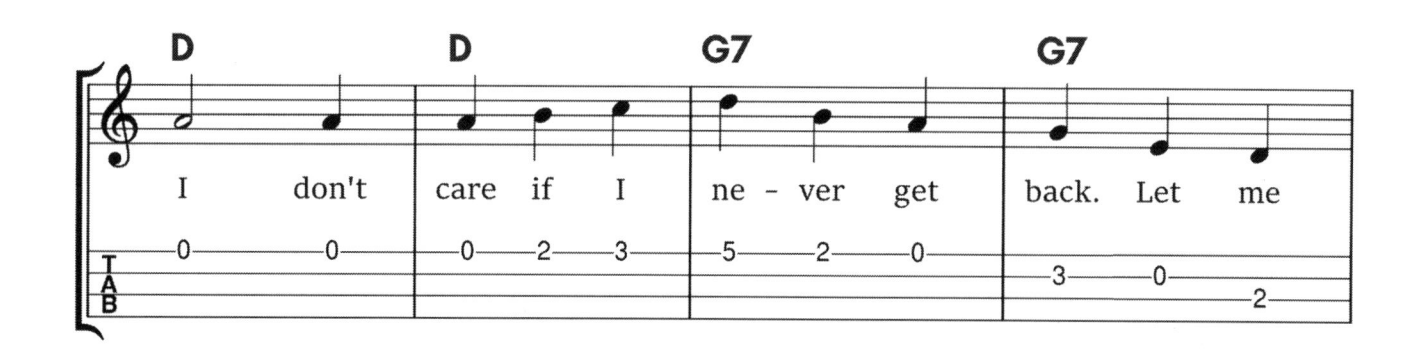

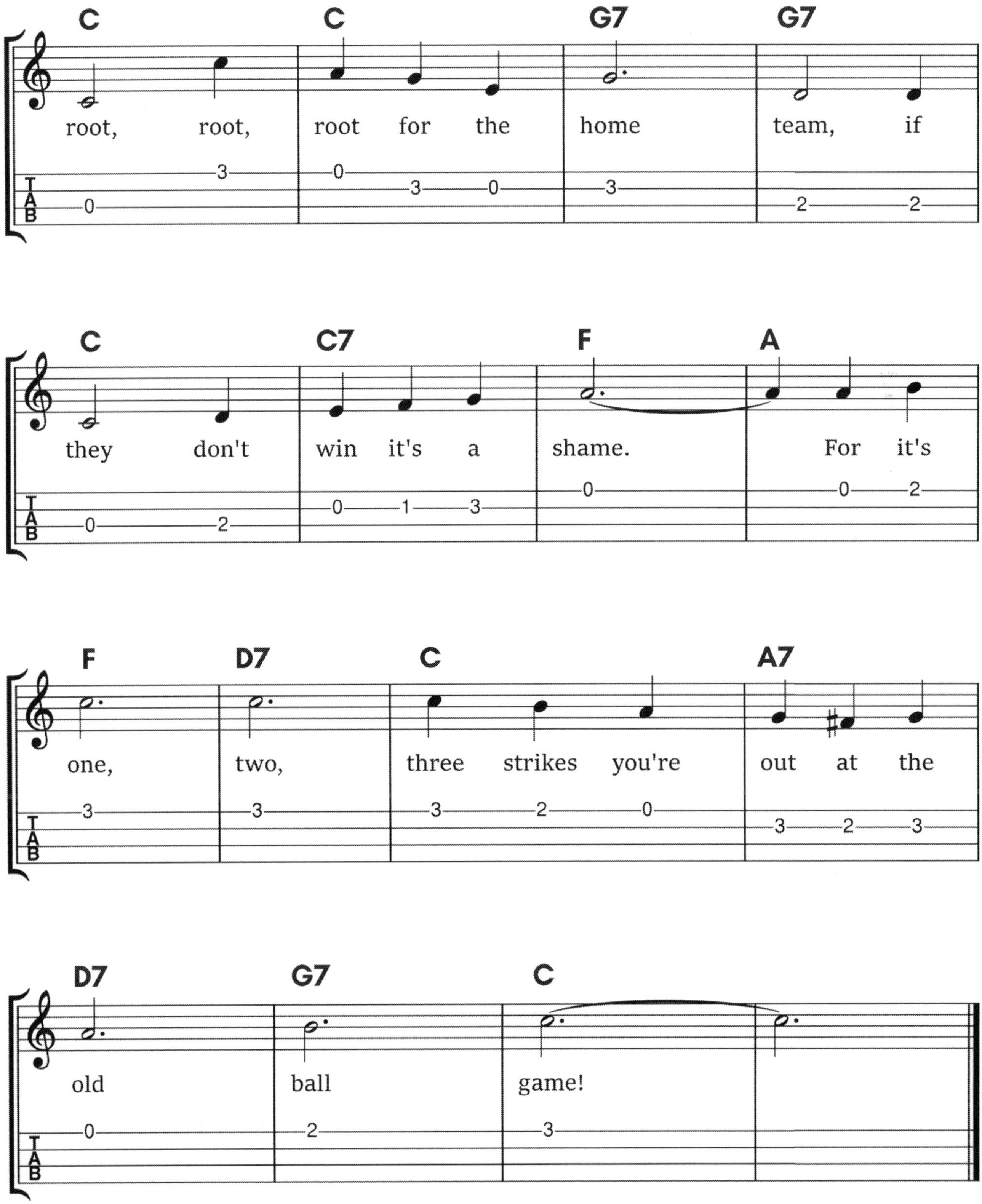
C C G7 G7
root, root, root for the home team, if
C C7 F A
they don't win it's a shame. For it's
F D7 C A7
one, two, three strikes you're out at the
D7 G7 C
old ball game!

Watch out for the tied eighth notes in the following tune. Pluck only the first note of each group of tied notes. Start with a slow count to figure out the rhythms.
1 and 2 and 3 and 4 and . . .

The chords of this fun little blues sound great with one strum, or any of the following strumming patterns. Try them all to see which one works best for you!

1. ↓ ↓ ↓ ↓
   1 2 3 4

2. ↓ ↓ ↓ ↓↑
   1 2 3 4

3. ↓ ↓↑ ↑↓↑
   1 2 3 4

Remember, it's OK to make mistakes! Regular practice is the key.

## U-kin' Blues

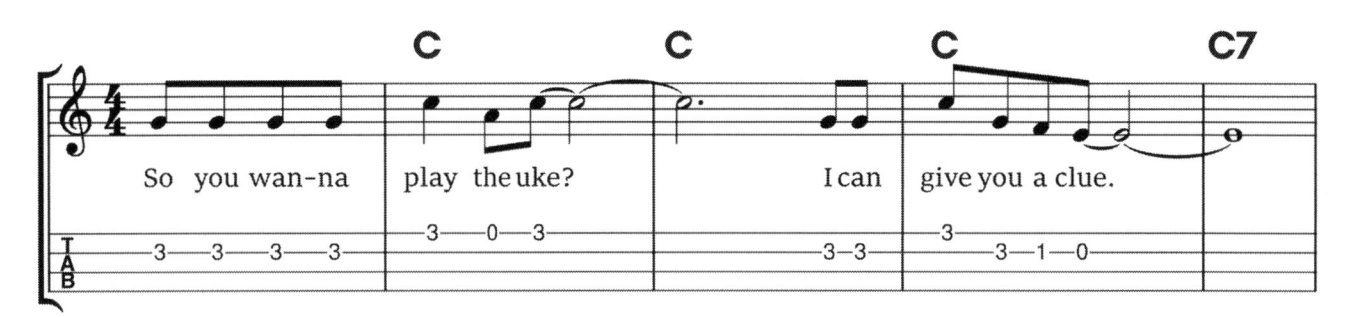

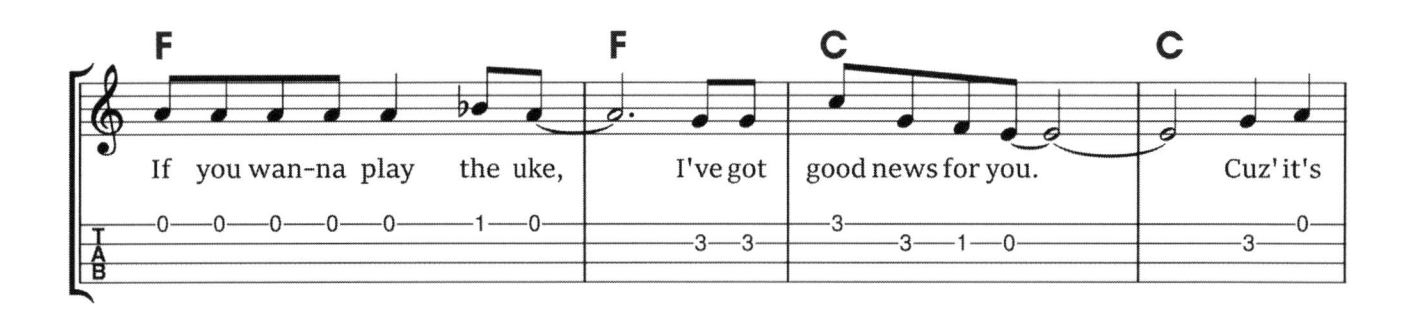

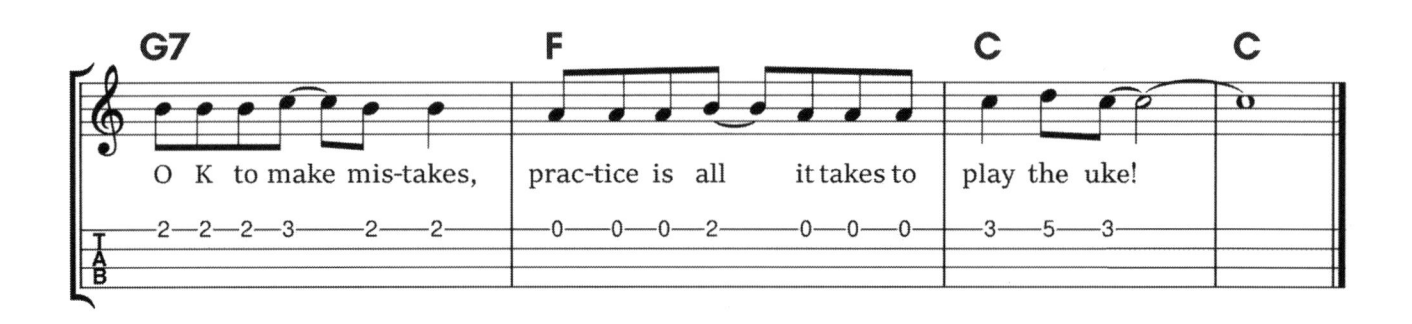

So you wan-na play the uke? I can give you a clue.

If you wan-na play the uke, I've got good news for you. Cuz' it's

O K to make mis-takes, prac-tice is all it takes to play the uke!

# THANK YOU!

Thank you SO much for purchasing and playing through **Ukulele for Beginners and Beyond**! I sincerely hope you got tons of value out of this book. It's the culmination of years of teaching, and countless hours of planning, writing, editing, layout and design.

If you found this to be a fun and useful tool on your musical journey, **please consider leaving a positive review on Amazon**. Help bring the JOY of music into homes all over the world. I'm proud to share that thanks to your support, more than 22,000 copies of my first four books have been sold worldwide!

Don't forgot to subscribe to my YouTube channel **Pierre Hache Music** for tons of FREE videos, including play alongs, chord hacks, practice tips and more.

I hope the skills you've developed here will allow you to learn and play more of the music you love. Some of the songs in this method have additional verses which are easily found online. The chords and lyrics to any popular songs you want to learn are a quick internet search away. And, when you come across any individual chords you don't know, you can look them up too.

Pick up your instrument as often as possible, keep discovering new music, play with other people and share the JOY of music.

Thanks again and Happy Playing!

*Pierre*

# ALSO FROM PIERRE HACHE MUSIC

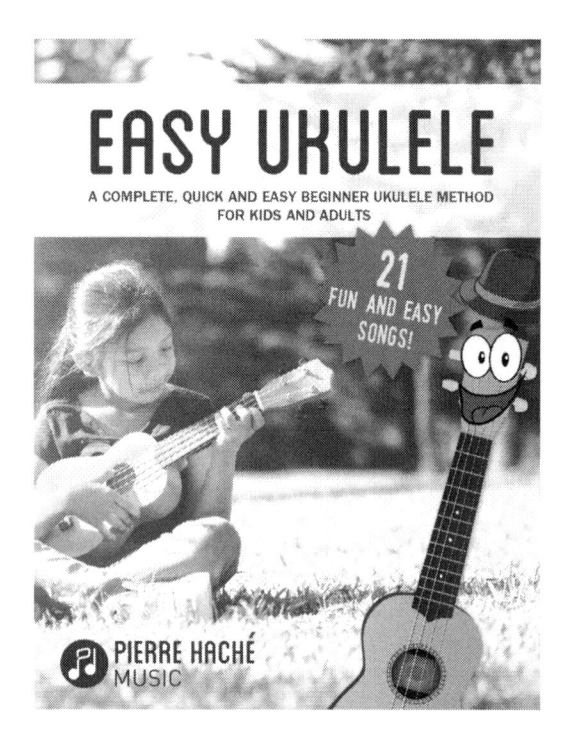

### Do You Want to Feel the JOY of Strumming and Singing?

*Easy Ukulele* makes it **FUN** and **FAST** with **FREE** Video Lessons to guide you!

This beginner ukulele book will teach you basic exercises, chords and rhythms, and before you know it, you'll be able to strum and sing 21 Fun Songs!

With more than **100 Free Videos** on the **Pierre Hache Music YouTube Channel** to complement the book, learning how to play the ukulele has never been easier!

### Listen, Learn and Play Your Way Through this Interactive Story for Kids!

Muse is both a touching tale about friendship, feelings and the power of imagination, and a fun introduction to rhythm and music for children ages 4 to 9.

The key musical concepts cleverly woven into the story apply to ANY instrument. Play creative clapping games, learn about melody and dynamics, read and write basic rhythms, and sing along as you join Lily and Muse in this one-of-a-kind dream-filled interactive children's book!

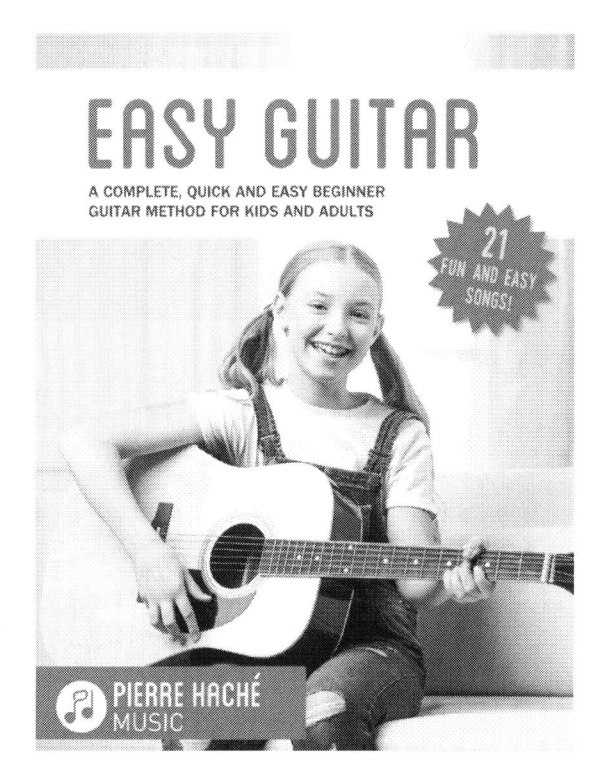

## Learning How to Play the Guitar Has Never Been Easier!

This complete, clear and concise guitar method and songbook takes you from simple children's music to playing your favorite pop songs!

It includes colorful pictures & diagrams, practice tips, essential chords, tons of songs, strumming patterns and more!

***Easy Guitar*** is the perfect companion for guitar lessons, or for learning on your own. Progress through these pages at your own pace, and most of all, Have Fun!

## Unleash Your Creativity With or Without a Drum Set!

Learn to read rhythm, play essential rudiments, familiar children's songs, classic rock grooves, exciting drum fills and even drum solos in this colorful drumming book!

Overflowing with pictures and diagrams, this step-by-step method is designed to keep the student's attention, encourage musicality and produce results. Based on more than 20 years of teaching experience, this unique approach provides hours of focused practice and play for anyone interested in the wide world of drumming.